I0489593

Scryptic

Magazine of Alternative Art and Literature

Issue 2.1

ISBN-13: 978-1721736157

ISBN-10: 1721736158

Dear readers and contributors,

Welcome to issue 2.1! With over 150 pages of art spanning multiple genres, this is the biggest issue of Scryptic to date. If you follow us on social media, you know that we're going to be implementing a few changes in our second year of publishing. The biggest change is moving into a bi-monthly publication schedule, meaning Scryptic will be published six times a year instead of four. Our main reason for doing this is the steadily increasing number of submissions we receive each period, and with all honesty, we've had to reject quite a few fantastic pieces that are more than worthy of being published simply because we can't fit everything we like into one issue. It is our hope that by publishing bi-monthly, Scryptic will become a more inclusive platform for artists and writers to share their darkest musings that would otherwise have a difficult time finding a home simply because of their content. We're also expecting the issues to be noticeably smaller because of this, offering a more intimate reading and viewing experience.

The other change we're going to implement is with our print issues. We have decided to publish print issues in black and white and color. This is all for you guys! This way, if you'd like to continue purchasing print editions in color, awesome! Go for it! However, for cost efficiency, we will also provide issues in black in white. This will cut the cost in half so that people with a limited budget will have access to a tangible copy!

Also, if you haven't heard, we are curating art and literature for a new anthology titled Group Therapy. Guidelines for this collection will be on the last page of this issue.

We really hope you enjoy issue 2.1!

All the best,
Chase and Lori

Just An Unhinged Lunatic Howling At The Moon

On a moonlit late night
I sat in a bar
Drinking drams of demented, fermented dream dew
Just an unhinged lunatic
Dreaming of howling at the full moon

Watching the world walk by
Looking at all the fine looking babes
Walking by the street
Thinking wild, erotic thoughts
Of endless wild libertine passions

When into the bar
Walked the most beautiful women
In the Universe
So wild, so free
So wonderfully alive

I did not know what to do
As this vision of delight
Sauntered through the bar
In a skin tight leather pants
Looked so fine
That my eyeballs hurt

And finally I had to say something
So I gathered up my manly courage
And walked up to her
And she looked at me
And instantly bewitched my soul
With a devilish grin
I lost all reason
And became a raving lunatic
Unhinged lunatic
Howling at the moon

Foaming at the mouth
A wild, free werewolf
Howling at the lunatic light
Of the full Moon

– Jake Cosmos Aller

God's Confession

I was sitting along
In a god forsaken bar
Somewhere on the lunatic fringes
Of society

On the bad part of town
Over by railroad tracks
Heading to hell
As fast as I could drink it down

Enjoying my lonely drink
Drinking by my lonesome self
With my partners
Jimmy Dean, and the Walker brother
And his old Granddad
Just drinking and hanging
With the Jack Daniel's gang

A crazed bum
With a thousand year stare
Walks up to me

He begins
Muttering to himself
Nutty nonsense
Crazy words
In a lunatic's voice

He had the look
Of one possessed
By his own demons
That only he can see
Or hear
Possessed by a secret knowledge
Only he knew

Despite myself
I was fascinated
By this lunatic's tale

So I stopped him
And said
So what's your game
Anyway

The short little dude
Stopped his insane prattle

Starting at me
With that thousand year old stare

Just another washed up
Lunatic
Too many drugs
Too many bad nights
On the wrong side of life

He looked at me
And proclaimed his story

He reared up
And filled up the room
And lifted the bar
On his finger
And stared down at me
From the sky

And said
Since you asked
I am God
The alpha and Omega
The real deal
The original dude of dudes
The sultan of Swing
God of hosts
And father of that Jesus dude

But no one knows me
Any more
No one cares
They think I am irrelevant
They think I am dead
They think I am a fairy tale
From some olden, ancient time

Some say I am dead
Others think I should be dead
That my work is done

I looked at him
Carefully now
And what did I see
An old man
With that lunatic look
But there was something else

He was crazy
Sure yes
But perhaps he was the real deal

I mean why not
Why would not God be
A lunatic wandering around loose
Talking to low lives like me
In a bar
On the way to hell

So I looked at him
And invited him to share
His tale of woe

God tells me
Well, it's like this

Many a year ago
People believed in me
But one day
They quit believing in me
And they went on without me

As they left me
My powers got weaker and weaker
And so eventually I became
What you see today

A broken down drunk
Hanging out
Looking for a hand out
Looking for some company
Or at least a free dinner

And he laughed and laughed
And I looked at him
And saw the beginnings of the end
And the ends of the beginnings

I saw a million planets
Flash by
A billion people
A trillion sentient beings
Thinking all at once
Thoughts filled my head
Lights flashed
And I knew
He was telling the truth

But it did not matter
In this day and age
Of materialism

God has no role
God is truly dead
And so I bought him a drink
And walked out of the bar
Profoundly sadden by what I had seen

God was dead
And we had all conspired
To kill him

Long live God

– Jake Cosmos Aller

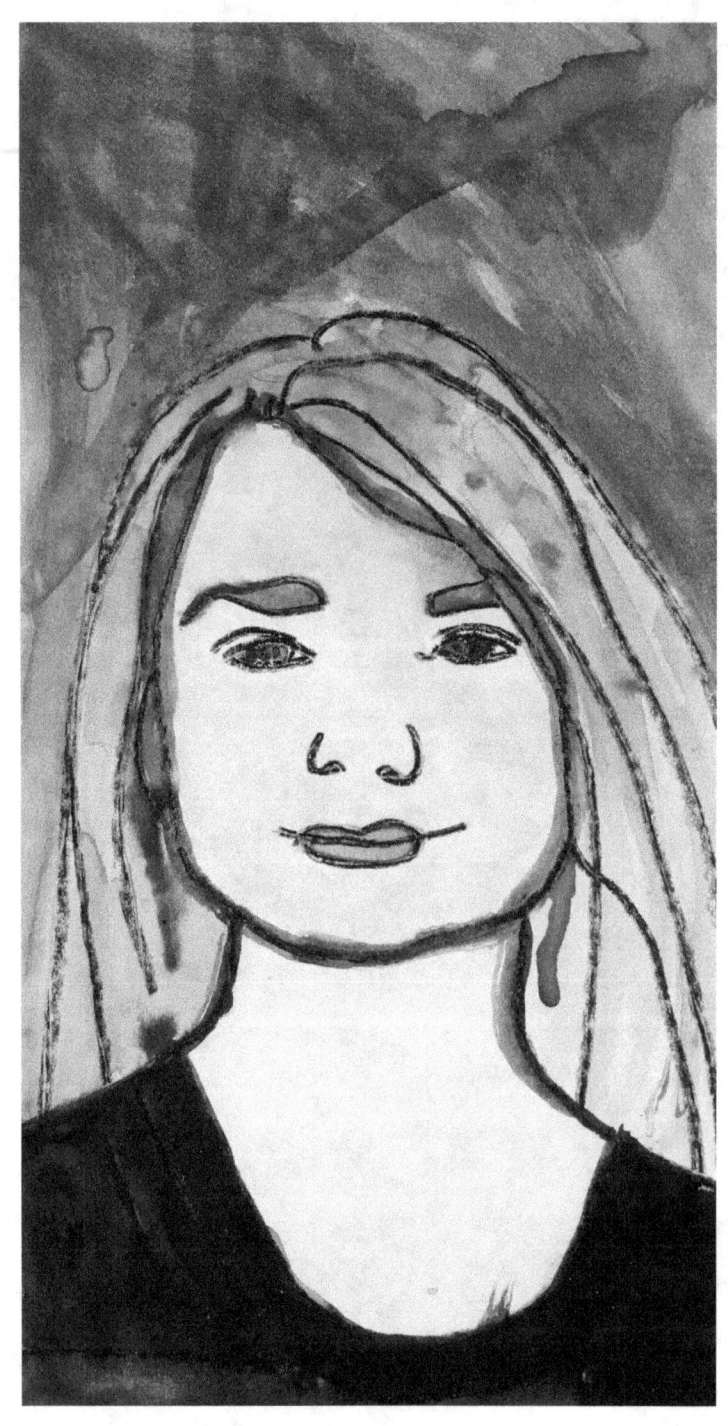

– Syd Little, age 11

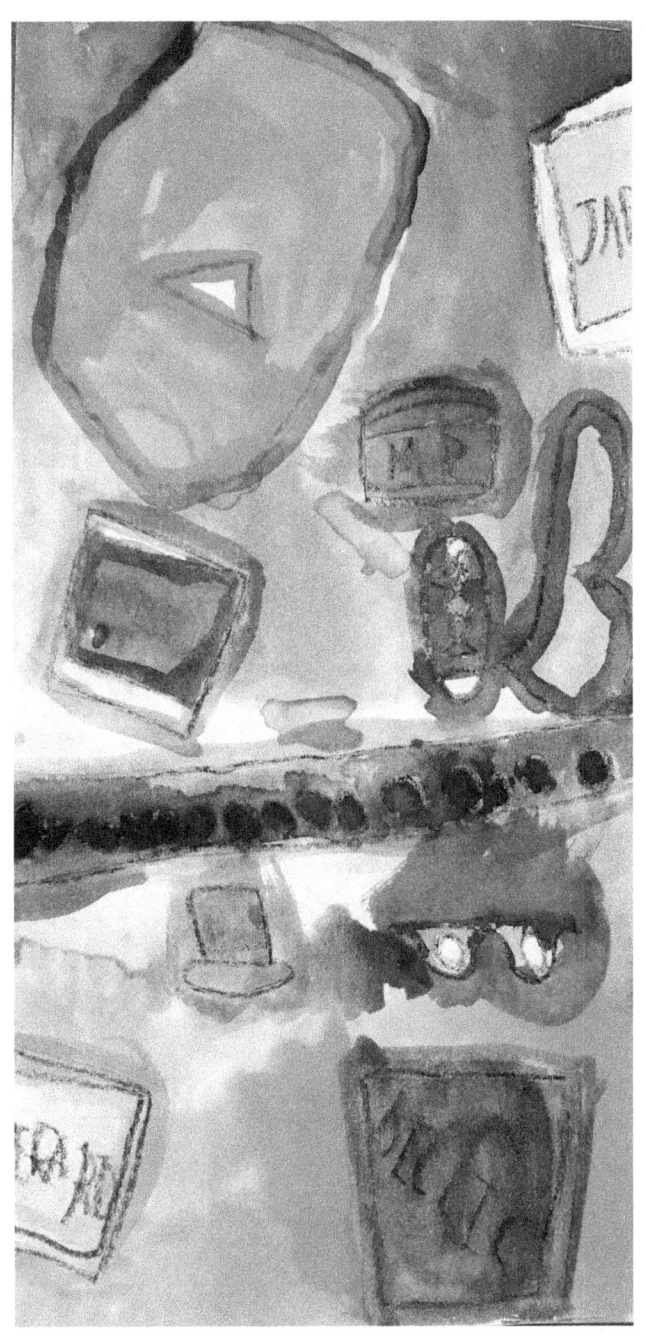

– Syd Little, age 11

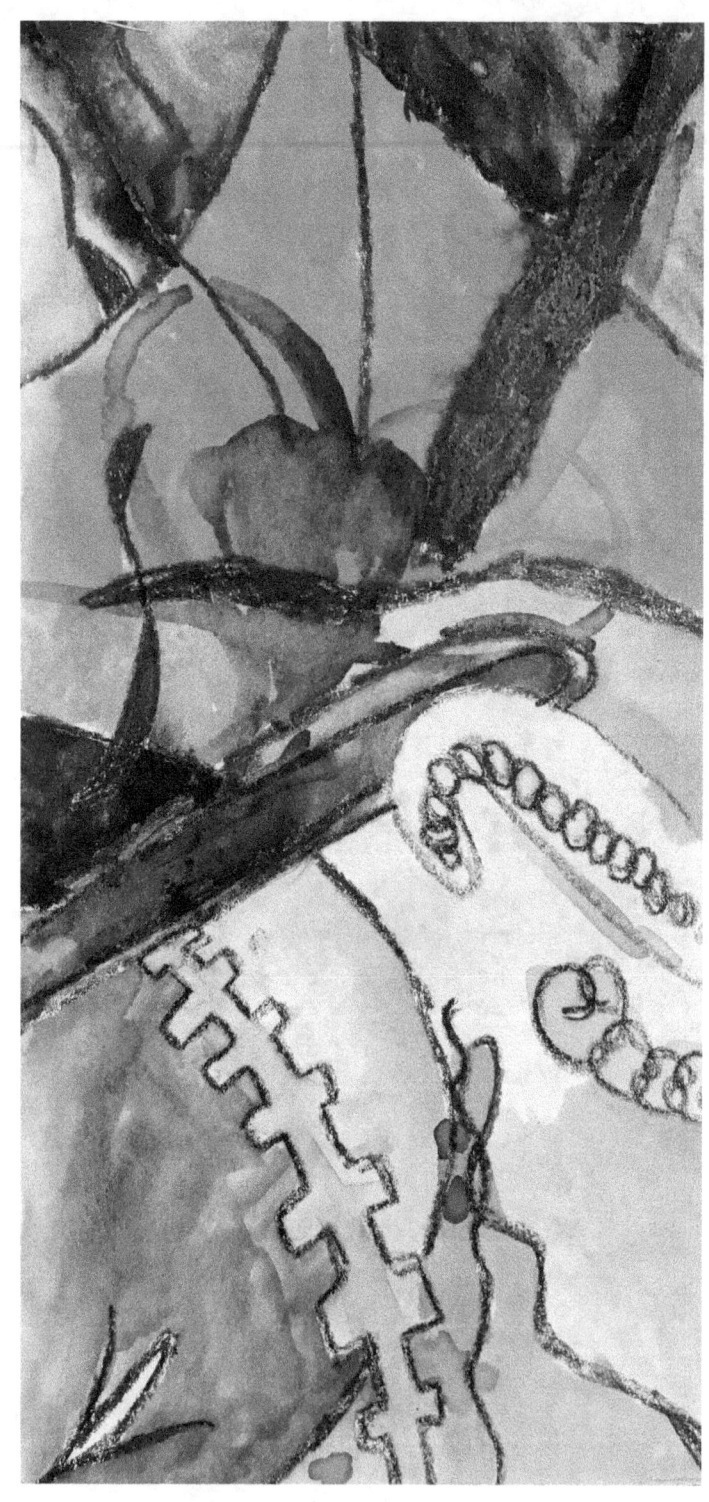

– Syd Little, age 11

suicide note
mist gathers around
the street light

sleepless night
a train drags the sun
into my day

– Bee Jay

Outside In

revival service
the way words
fall into our wallets

altar call
I check the dip
of my neckline

demonic oppression
my statements
turn to questions

laying on of hands
the slight pass
over my bra strap

born again
what I love
becomes sin

a test
of my faith
biology 101

group prayer
how we keep up
with the joneses

daily devotions
all the ways
I'm undone

repentance
not enough
hot coals

deconversion
sunday mornings
now my own

– *Tia Haynes*

waiting

I watch the yolk break and run into the egg white. They don't know that I've spent the morning fighting back tears of depression. I call out that breakfast will be ready soon and ask them what they want to drink. Watching the eggs bubble I wonder if I should have ever had children at all. Strawberries sit on the cutting board and the bread bag is still twisted shut. I stand in the kitchen fighting against the winter and the dark and the cold. The kids wander in and start pulling their plates off the counter. And I pull on my smile.

cloudy night
how my shadow
hides

present and accounted for

Sitting in the nursery, reading all your current favorites, we sink deeply into one another. This moment, while your whole body still fits snugly into my lap, makes me almost forget. Your weight, your warmth, is a balm to my mind. I almost forget the pills I take three times a day. The days I'm not sure I can do this any longer. The weeks, months, years, spent dancing on the edge of madness. Here, the seconds expand into lifetimes. I have yet to disappoint you. Yet to become someone you no longer recognize. Yet to be a source of shame. I am still the one you run to after you fall. Still the one you call for in the middle of the night. Still mama. I am not what I was, I'm not what I will be, I am who you believe me to be; safe and sound.

locked door
the way my nurse says
"good night"

beyond the pale

It was days after our daughter's birth that we decided to leave. We set up an exit strategy that took months of careful negotiation to pull off. Explanations of theological differences were cited. Lies about being "called to the workforce and out of ministry" were given. Anything we could grab at we did. The truth was that we couldn't look at our baby and see God anymore. At least not their god.

folded pamphlet
I follow the preacher's
snakeskin shoes

– Tia Haynes

lost miracles

We weren't trying to get pregnant. It wasn't until the anatomy scan that we knew she would be alright despite the Lithium.

unexpected guest
I sweep the dirt
under the rug

Hours after birth they pull her off my breast. The medication we thought was safe, still isn't.

fresh basil
with every cut
a bruise

As I stand at the sink mixing formula, my eyes settle on the middle distance.

postpartum depression
even her cries
can't reach me

legacy

Everyone else had left. We had packed up all we could not knowing when the bank would come and repossess the condo. Grimy from the months of disuse, your final home held nothing for me. The home we moved into after the divorce. The home I discovered how to smoke in. The home I had my own affair in. Now, standing at the bottom of the steps with a last sweeping look around, I whisper "did you ever love me?"

slush
these worn shoes
still holding on

– Tia Haynes

vodka hangover
lost on
the tundra

– *Julian O'Dea*

these fears
the unreached depths
of the lake

night of your passing
a single star
fills the sky

just waiting
for the darkness
hidden memories

that argument again
the crack
of thin ice

twisted branches
in the twilight
how I shiver

broken
my story scrawled
in red

another IV
silent drops fall
from my face

searching for you
each grave leads deeper
into the mist

lilies opening the pain of your absence

your birthday again
all the candles
you'll never light

– *Rachel Sutcliffe*

How Trouble Grows

Trouble is patient
hiding around corners.
creeping through shadows
entering without a sound.

It starts as a seed blown
by careless winds and
covers your garden with
foul brackish weeds.

Or sparks from a match
spread over fertile ground
becoming flames speeding
through the long night.

Trouble knows where you live.
You cannot hide from it.
Gaining a foothold, growing
fat feeding on your flesh.

Watch how trouble grows
inch by inch, molecule
by molecule coursing
through your veins.

Trouble begins as a whisper
day by day growing louder.
Now your heart beat becomes
a thumping drum.

Soon you will forget
there was a time
when trouble was
not at your side.

– Joan McNerney

Silenced

What is never spoken of, pushed down,
becomes mold crawling over hearts.

Strangling our voices, it scuttles through
corridors, tunneling, warping each day.

My body, this swollen thing carried by
legs too thin and crippled to uphold it.

Pushed down, tightly clamped in,
full of pain, gasping for each breath.
Smothered now.

– Joan McNerney

divination by:
a cycle of five poems

Aichmomancy: by sharp objects

How far up can I drop the pin, the spear, the record needle
before it slices through dermis into adipose, into viscera?
Or do I just remember it sinking deeper as a child?
(Aren't I always the child?) The recordings of words
spoken or refused continue to darken the snow
with ancient crimes, and anticoagulants
are so ineffective this near
the orchestra.

– Scott Ferry

Brontomancy: by thunder

As General Subutai surrounds the city
of Kaifeng, the Jin soldiers ignite the fuses
of the strange iron globes. Silvergrass
instantly evaporates, moist chests
wrapped in gleaming armor separate into sound.
Ears concuss, eyes black with chalk. The disturbance
carries across from Mongolia, to Europe, to Japan,
to Vietnam, to Iraq, to Syria; to bus stations,
restaurants, schools, nightclubs,
mosques. The lightning blinds and deafens
still. Motionless, we wait for another light
under the flying hail.

– Scott Ferry

Grammomancy: by writing individual letters

Letters, left alone, like bare numerals,
infarct, sew chords into themselves
by virtue of hunger. No phone, no internet,
almost as tragic as no family. A sea squirt
can rewrite its entire body with just
a fragment of blood vessel, a long vowel,
maybe oo, or even oui. A Ouija board
only points to one letter at a time. Then it
becomes possible to piece together
meaning from a string of swift stops.
But I never ask the planchette
specifically when I will die. And I have
been warned to never touch the plastic disk alone.
They can take over. There have been
isolated instances of plates and shoes
streaking across rooms to strike doors.
Who are they? Are there theys watching
behind a screen for a single fingerpad to graze
the small sliding heart? And why would they
be honest with my future? Would they
see a slideshow of isolated strokes,
peppermint chocolate spilled on the cracked
dashboard, sunscreen smeared after the sand
snapped the vertebrae? Could they read aloud
my whole sentence, spelling out each
f a l l through the veil?

– Scott Ferry

Hydatoscopy: by rainwater

Mist: not enough to gamble on, keep the eucalyptus
hips hidden in a murmur of curses, don't open
your lips to even breathe

Drizzle: the words lengthen, laryngospasm, mild
dyspnea as the mucilage dots the tongue
it may be possible to capture a fly

Sprinkle: this is more like crying, if antifreeze
on the street shines sweetly, then drive erratically
around churches

Rain: digestive phrases leak heavy onto coffee cups
from the rust playing on balconies, h. pylori
ulcerates eventually

Cats: rafters give way and iguanas dig talons into my mastoid
as they dance down

Dogs: destroy slender tomato starts which poke out of the groin
like inaccurate depictions of joy

Tropical: swim along, leach, attach to ankles, try to remember when
the wounds weren't there

Deluge: it was the end of the last ice age not rain
your Neanderthal auntie skinny dipped in the fjords
of Languedoc

– Scott Ferry

Umbromancy: by shade

Morning: coal and salt in my eyes when my bright object
moves away from me, like a drowning mother

Noon: nothing or everything is either clear or obscured,
work to build stalactites from hours of grim focus

Evening: forgive and give out candy termites on sticks
tell stories of how the darkness used to cover the others, the young

Night: the lightest phase of the moon, where the crater Langrenus
pours dead relatives into a rich broth with absinthe noodles, it tastes like home
a home I'd forgotten I already had

– Scott Ferry

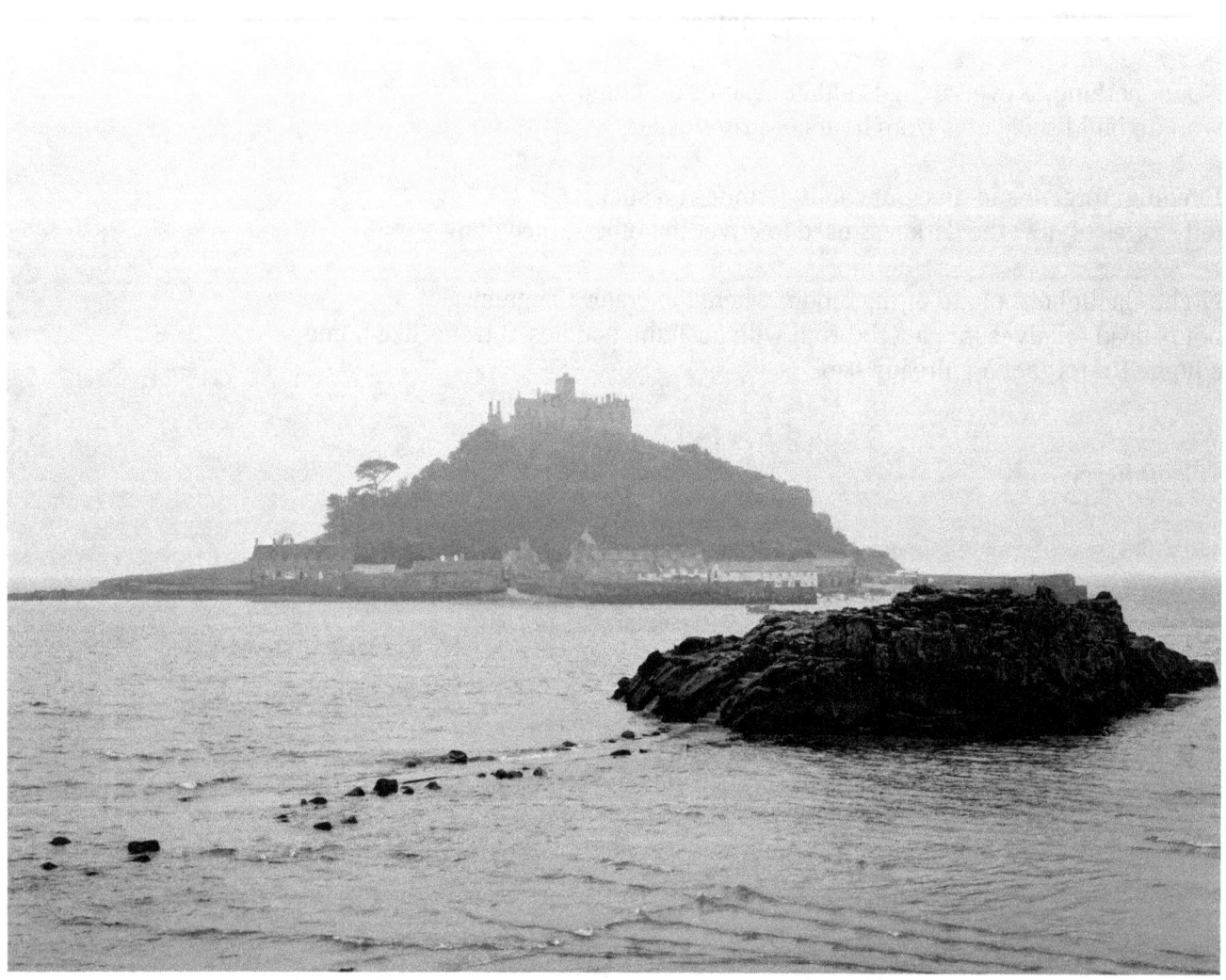

Fog

– Olivier Schopfer

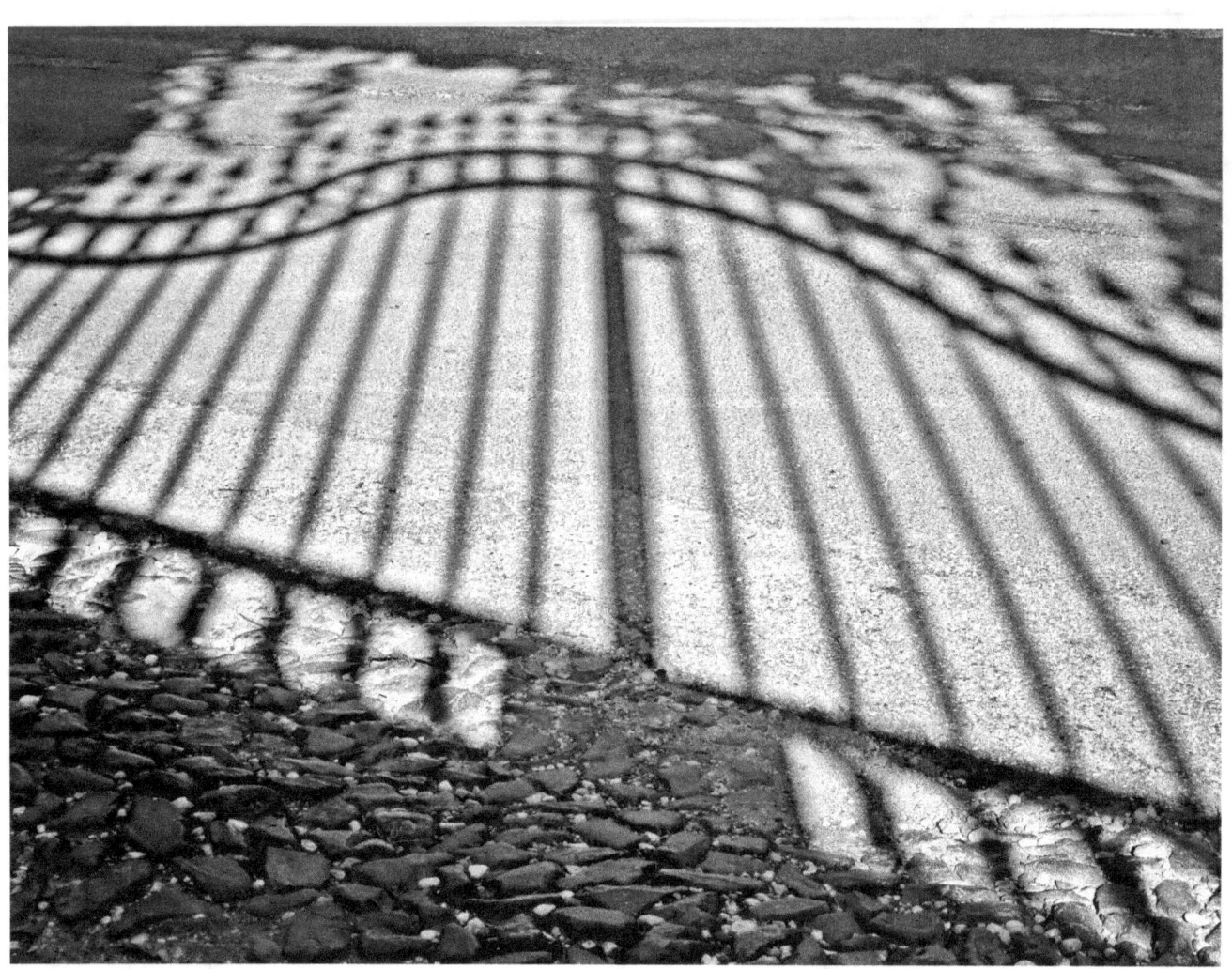

Shut In

– Olivier Schopfer

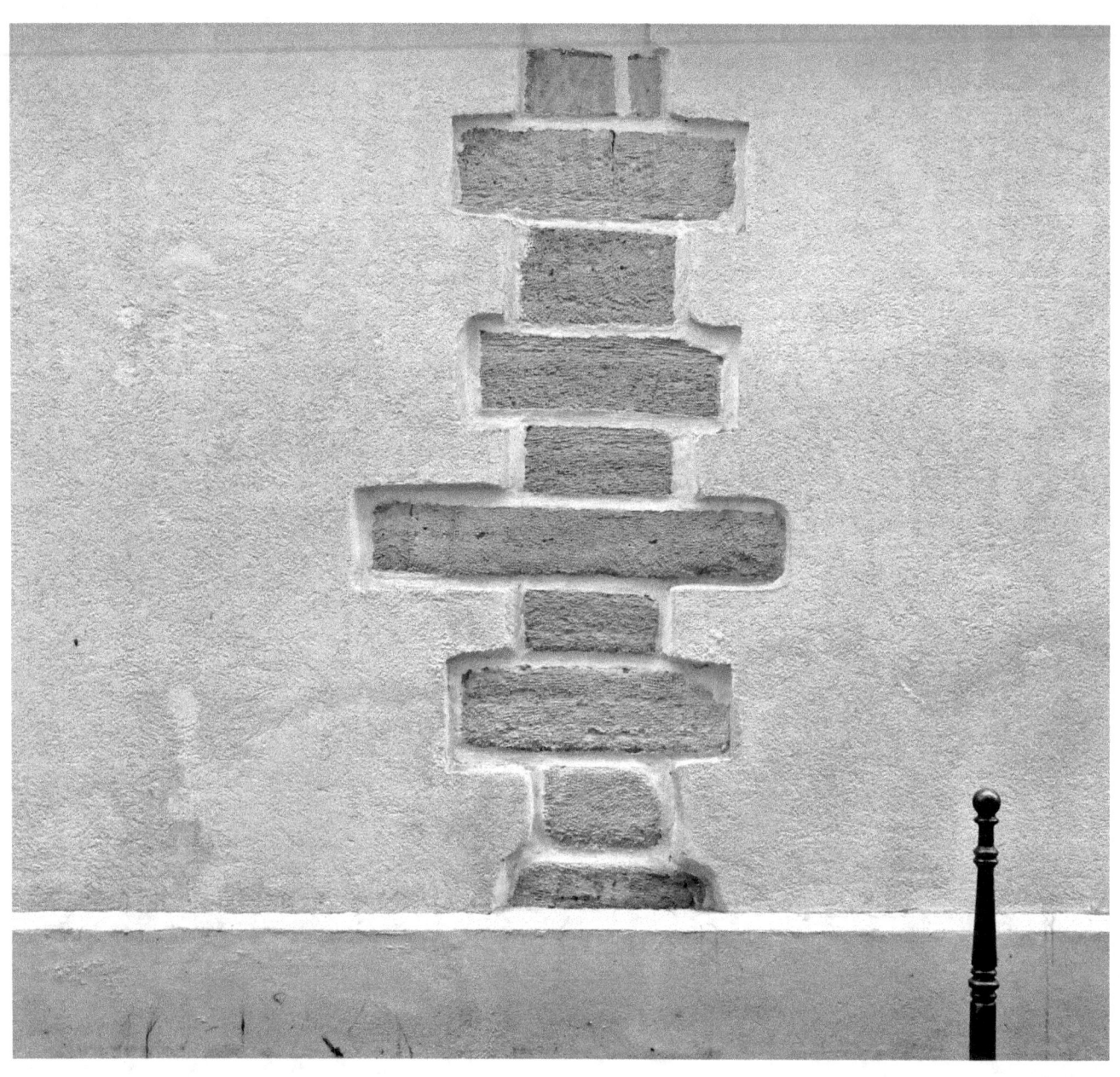

Scars

– Olivier Schopfer

Opening Door Syndrome

I accidentally slapped my hand on invisible instruments,
in the upstairs hallway, by the railing,
before I circus tumbled down the spiral staircase
and my head ended up in a gutter with paint cans.
As Saturday afternoon winds and hangs its
ticking sweat towel up to dry,
I run out to catch the mailman in a flash,
hear the boxcar putt-putting and
hook my boomerang overdue bill at 'em.
But first I have these new linen socks
to put on,
like a pen gliding across
clean paper.

– Alyssa Trivett

The Hospital That Day

Hell is cold here, for today.
I aligned myself along several park benches
after learning of your passing,
staring into the sun, burning out a retina
of tears.
I see the corpse I wanted to start
with my car battery
but my hands shake and the tools I need
wouldn't work in this situation.
I wore your watch and drove your car,
the next day. The chaplain shook my hand,
and gave me his business card.
Strangely enough,
I cannot remember his name.

– Alyssa Trivett

The Ghost Gang

I sneak off during the play to our meeting place under the skull mural. You're late as usual; we begin the search for Humphrey thirty minutes before the interval. Everyone knows the story of his tragic suicide after being dropped for the summer season of 1920. He's been the subject of our paranormal investigations since he pulled the Genie's trousers down on stage last Christmas.

spiral stairs
a sudden drop
in temperature

The balcony is deserted and cold this evening. Our motion detectors fail to reveal any supernatural activity so we move downstairs to scour the backstage area. Applause echoes through the corridors making it hard to pick up any spirit voices on the recording equipment.

dressing room
the ghost costume
fools no-one

The interval draws near as we climb steps to the VIP box. It provides a fine view of the Edwardian architecture. Scanning the audience, I notice a curtain move in the box on the other side of the theatre. A young clown appears and applauds the performance.

the drama
of mask shadows
stealing scenes

The clown waves his hands like a conductor. On his command an army of creatures crawl from the darkness. The building starts to shake and scarlet walls crumble. Debris falls into the audience; gargoyles gorge themselves on human flesh.

showstopper
final curtain call
on the empty stage

– Tim Gardiner

Metrosexual

To the gothic countess applying her lippy on the Hammersmith line this morning, a short poem:

mind the gap
between us...
the sweet smell
of your perfume
lingers

Perhaps we could meet up some time for a beverage, write some poems. I'd love a muse. Anon.

– Tim Gardiner

Homeland's Siege

It was mid-day in April
when the city was soaked in sulfur and blood.
The streets were a sepulcher of butchered men;
the smell of bullets and bombs perfumed the entire place.
Horrific wailings were heard everywhere;
cries of terror,
shouts of commiseration,
sighs of desperation:
All of them echoed in a city of ruins,
in a place of punished innocence and cold feet.
Loud shots were fired;
loads of canons roared like thunder.
From behind, heads were plucked from crime-less necks.
My knees shook; my palms breathed with ice.
The bandits were heading toward my direction;
I pleaded, "Good Lord! Let mercy reign..."
And it did.
Faith has shut the mouth of death.

– *Irish D. Torres*

Shakes and Storms

On a dark and stormy night,
pangs of hunger hugged me so tight.
The wild wind blew westward, shaking our old and rugged hut.
Raindrops filled the holes of our thin roof;
chills of the dripping rain fell under my skin.
I was shaking both in hunger and terror;
my stomach's rocking like gongs and cymbals.
Living in the dim outskirts of storm and famine
is the scariest horror movie ever launched.
The thunder roared loudly; the lightnings flashed.
Our roof shook as if it wanted to fly thousand miles away;
But that stormy night was not yet our dead end,
for tonight, the ghost-storm is visiting us again.
As I'm writing this, the flood reaches me at knee-length.
The wind keeps blowing the light of my four-inch candle.
I doubt if I could finish writing this poem tonight
but believe me!
I am able to scribble the 18th line amidst this monstrous cyclone.

– *Irish D. Torres*

mouthless teddy bear
a mother stitches on
her own smile

wendigo tea party
a three year old
serves biscuits

play therapy
the monster
she's become

scrubbing ancient skulls
my own eyes
fill with mud

tracing the bones
of an unlived life
flower impressions

– Lucy Whitehead

Stanley's Creation

Stanley
was a brakeman
in Jersey City
for Western Railroad
who beat his wife Anna,
a devout Irish Catholic
from Dublin
who beat their son Richard
so hard with a broom handle
that she often broke the handle
and had to buy a new broom,
and when Stanley whipped the boy
he used a belt or other household
instruments claiming the child
had fallen down a flight of stairs
when the doctors grew suspicious
so that when Richard was older
he kept killing his father over
and over again
except the people he killed
were not his father
and the people that paid him
to kill always marvelled
at his stone cold
proficiency.

– Ryan Quinn Flanagan

Milkman

I am the milkman.
I am the now
man.

No way around it.
Heroin sleep man.

Skyscraper short man.
You wouldn't believe it.

Opium Samuel poem man.
Back at Abyssinia school again.

Evening tutorial
walk home dizzy in the
rain man.

Run a bath
run a marathon,
competitive rehydrating
man.

You are the birds.
I hear you prison sing.

Between the leafy green hours
along the footpath of my
constant wet walking.

– Ryan Quinn Flanagan

Sin Bin

Who wants to be innocent?
Not me.

I want to be guilty of some things at least.

Not the biggies that get you put away,
but many of the others would be nice.

Don't tell me you are innocent.
Everyone is guilty of something.
Which is fine.

Ignore the sin bin crazies.
They believe Noah and his ark full of animals
were the world's first carpoolers.

Cheated on your diet, guilty.
Jaywalked across a deserted street at four in the morning, guilty.
"I did not have sexual relations with that woman,"…guilty.
How many little white lies have you told just today?
To keep the peace and some basic working order?

I don't want to be innocent.
Innocence is a lie.

I want to be guilty and alive.
Enjoying the few pleasures we get
for the short time we are here.

Didn't read all of War and Peace, guilty.
Toilet papered cars, guilty.
Found $20 on the ground and kept it, guilty.
Impure thoughts…haha, where to start!

Shoplifted food when I was starving, guilty.
Call in sick when I am not sick, guilty.
Give out false numbers at bars, guilty.
Said I loved you when I didn't, guilty…

– *Ryan Quinn Flanagan*

Ruins

I guess ruins have to be ancient
for people to want to go stand in them.
Pay admittance and fly whole continents
to do so.

When a fire or some other horrible disaster happens here,
nobody pays to stand inside the ruins.

They deem it unsafe
and knock the damn
thing down.

And argue with the insurance companies
that never pay and always have an out.

And no one call them ruins.
Even though that is what they are.
They call it a tragedy.
Hardly ever stopping to smile
for selfies.

– Ryan Quinn Flanagan

Body Slam

wrestling
with the angels
of others
is never fruitful

they are hardly
even angels

more like
sleep from your eye
that you whisk away
with the back of
your hand

crinkling your way
through bubble wrap boxes
that have come through
the mail

never a pipe bomb inside,
though you'd be fine with that

or some fine powder
like leaving a crematorium
full of pet names

life should be a clumsy celebration
of circumstance
where the living never wrestle
with the dead or their
angels

surrounded by books and moments
and bottles music moments

kisses in the dark
under strange carnivorous
blankets.

– *Ryan Quinn Flanagan*

Rorschach test
the ink that runs through
my veins

refusing my breast crack baby's wail

trainspotting
dirty syringes litter
the playground

graffiti
I trace the mind of
an artist

– Veronika Zora Novak

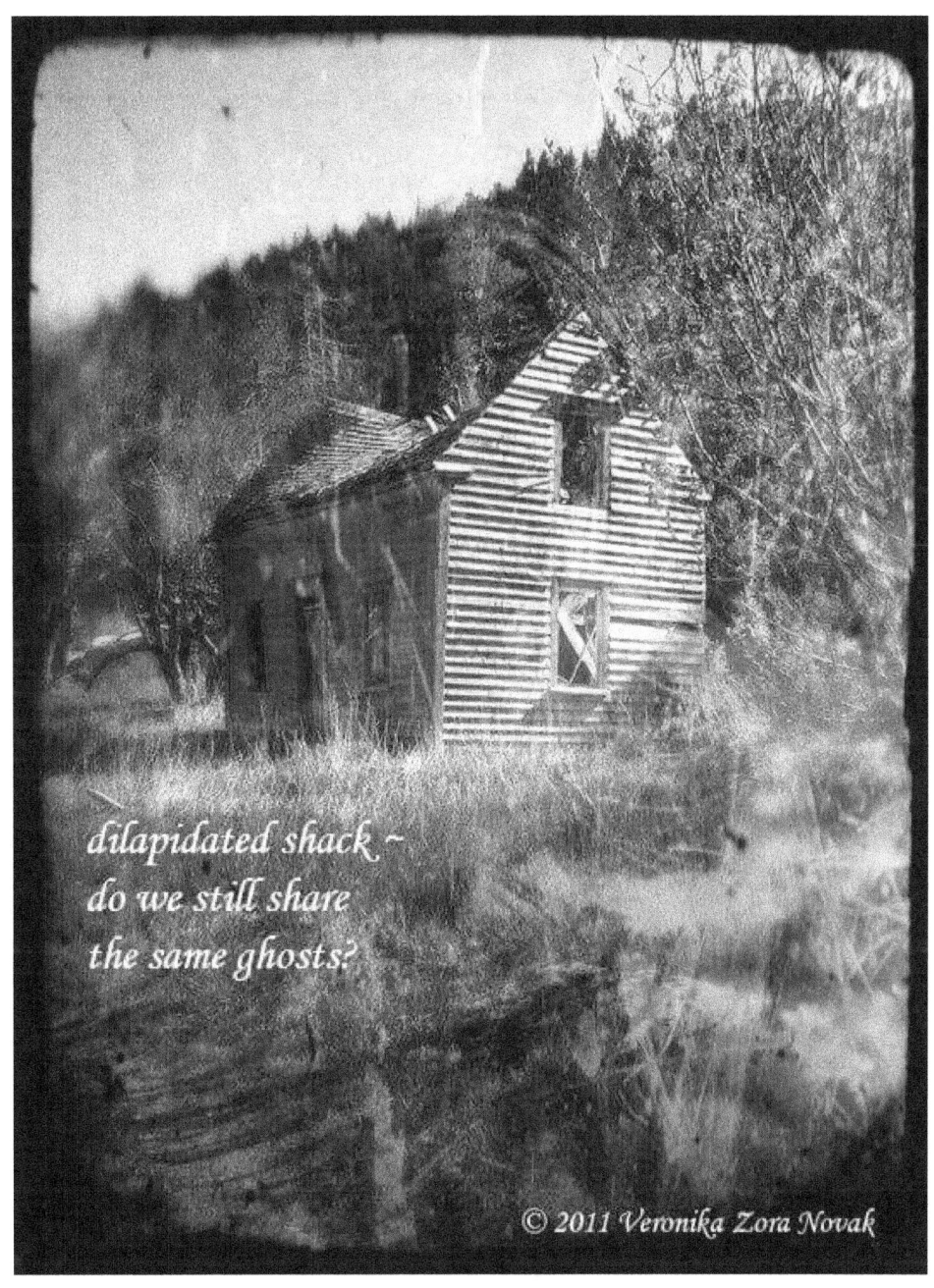

dilapidated shack ~
do we still share
the same ghosts?

– Veronika Zora Novak

barren womb...
winter's desolation
in her bones

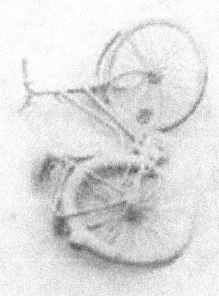

Veronika Zora Novak

How's This for Fucked-Up

Now that my sister's dead, I'm rich. I call it a mercy killing, because I really need the cash. Getting her insurance money was easy. The other part, living with her, was hell. I earned that million.

I think of all the things I can do now. Provide clean water to 500 villages in Africa. Put happy smiles on 10,000 children with deformed lips. Put 100 poor kids through college. Clone Charlie, my toy poodle, who's got this throat thing that's fatal.

I like the cloning idea. But should I get two Charlies at a time or start with one and when that Charlie dies get the next one? I'm only 35. I have another 50 years ahead of me. And Charlie had 10 good years. So that means...oh, I can't figure it out. Or decide what to do.

I wish I could ask my sister about cloning Charlie. She was good at telling me what to do. She excelled at it. That was one of her favorite words. She loved being Miss Bossy Boots. Getting all up in my business. You excel at picking losers she's say. Like Joe. She never liked Joe. Just because he hangs around schoolyards. Turns out was right about him. That asshole sniffed out my 13 year old dog-walker. My sister never shut up about it. She could have stopped with Joe. But she had to name all the other losers I'd slept with going back as far as Richie. Dumb jock, par excellence. That's what she called Richie. And she'd say it in this phony French accent. Anyway, that's when I started thinking. How easy it would be. Figuring out how to kill her wasn't hard. I stole the poison cannoli idea from Talia Shire. Godfather III. But it was all for nothing. My sister slipped and fell in the shower. Broke her neck, the doctor said. Life's funny like that.

Now that she's gone I feel all weird and adrift. A word I never thought I'd use. Adrift. Like a tiny rowboat without an anchor. She would have figured out how many Charlies to clone, how much to spend on each one, and how much of her insurance money I'd have left over. To live on. She wouldn't even need to write it down, she'd do it all in her head. If only I could ask her. That and a bunch of other stuff. Which is why I'm thinking of getting her cloned. The million should just about cover it. Or I could go for the robot-relative option. That's only half a mil. Lots of cash leftover and me telling her what to do. A win-win. I think it's the best idea I've ever had. Par excellence.

– *Roberta Beary*

Hush Little Baby

Today my little girl is at the playground without her big sister. I can't stop looking at her. It's hard to see the whole playground from my window. I'm not supposed to go near the playground. The judge said so. The judge understands how much I love little girls with long hair. That's why I can't go near the playground. I need the little girl to sit on my lap. So I can braid her hair. I won't do anything else. I won't play rocking horse with her hair. I won't even if she wants me to. Or maybe I will. Maybe she'll like me playing rocking horse. She looks like she might like it. I think she can see me. Waving at her. She's waving back. I'll just go get her now. So I can braid her hair. While she sits on my rocking horse. She'll like it. I promise.

– Roberta Beary

Nocturnal Souls

Those pure, breathable love-notes
written on Japanese paper.
Our house, rain-cold
with dawn dying in every corner.

When you sleep
I believe I am made of ice. I travel
in my frozen figure, spiraling,
drilling up
into God's domain. While you, flat
amongst the covers, breathe slow like
roots, touchable, sacred
as the shadows of my mortality are born
then perish in the wind's mute philosophy.
Loneliness infects us all. You have told me,
there will never be a simpler tomorrow.

Cut flowers lean their bloom on pale walls.
I drop my mouth like wine dripped
on your shoulder.
You wake and find me,
hauntingly yours.

– *Allison Grayhurst*

Kaita

It is sort of colourless,
the Earth. Though
I can hear the voice of spring,
I cannot help being disappointed at the slow
blooming flowers, that grow up
pursing the sun
to no avail.
Then I see the long boneless bodies
of angels
ascending like arrows
into the depths of a starless sky,
and I think to myself that he
who has gone into
shadows, hissing a private song
is much better off with his visible scars than
their invisible wings.
And I wonder, will he come home
or pass like water between unwebbed feet, to the ocean
where all that is written
is washed away with the sand?

– Allison Grayhurst

When He Rides

Unearthly dreams
illuminate him
where gardens
lay their petals to rest.
They creep now, his eyes,
into sad and forbidden
realms
of insanity's broken weight.

Loose threads
dangling from his mind.
Loose thoughts
that have no ending.
Lost on his lips, something
unleashed like music, something
like my love.

> Find me alone
> inside bedroom walls,
> take these useless hands,
> allow them to touch
> the impossible

He makes the bell ring
He turns the lights off
He takes the bareback horse
and gallops
into the cutting dark.

The stars, they say,
lose all balance
when he rides.

– Allison Grayhurst

Freeze

Having just moved, I'm hunting for a new psychotherapist. Researching the potential candidates from my insurance website, I don't find much additional information, so I choose the lady whose Facebook profile picture is a green M&M. I accept this as a sign that she doesn't take herself too seriously. My only concern is she's a trauma expert but that isn't an issue for me. I'm just hoping she's adept at other conditions as well.

the density of mental illness   gravity anomaly

To some, I imagine her office is considered cozy. For me, it's like sharing a coffin with a stranger. I have to try really hard to not panic and run out. While she looks over my paperwork, I stare at the angel nightlight on the wall opposite me, wishing I had those wings. Increasingly anxious, I begin scanning every detail of the room in attempt to find a mental escape.

convergent boundaries   the sweat begins to flow

The therapist starts by asking why I've come and what I hope to achieve. All I know is that I'm supposed to be here and I don't want to die. She begins the scripted inquiry I've heard dozens of times until she suddenly stops and tilts her head.
"What was that?" she asks.
"What?" I respond, my eyes glancing at her and then quickly looking away again.
"You just paused and changed position, and facial expressions, as if reacting to something. What was it?"
"I don't know. Sometimes I just get…stuck."

someone from the inside screams   subglacial eruption

Suddenly, her line of questioning pivots and she poses questions I haven't been asked since I was first diagnosed, despite seeing numerous practitioners over the past twenty-five years.
Do you experience this? Do you do that?
"Yes! And yes! I've been telling them this for years!"
Finally, she asks about abuse and instead of lying as I did previously, I start to tell the truth.

stratigraphy   layer by layer I uncover my past

– *Robin Smith*

Mrs. Green's scattered brain...
the claw of a hammer

yet another failure suicide attempt

abandoned insane asylum...
before my diagnosis

– Robin Smith

Plaid Hands

after the massacre, the remaining bones were gathered,
placed into a pit and burned,crushed with rocks
their purpose served,offered as a sacrifice
to the god of abraham on bents knees basking in the light
of the razor man, he was a gentleman who had plaid hands
his skin was beige and he had no face,even without lips
he talked at great lengths, when the women are sleeping
he creeps into their beds, caressing their genitals
before eating their heads and flying back home
to his skeletons and chemicals, sticky black
substances pour out of his lap, an influx of his
spores laying a trap, the poisonous scent
crept slowly in the air, he slept knowing
they wept when voyeur-less. the joyfulness
he felt as he climbed on his horse, it's fur soaked in blood
from the coming war, nostrils flaring flames, fire
where there should be eyes, a mane made of blue flames
the heavens surrounded by a swarm of flies, astounded
by the sights he stretched his plaid hands towards the skies
plucking the stars away one by one, rearranging them
near our sun, with a kick of his feet he unleashed his steed
and rode around the earth in a manner of minutes
once he was finished the horse ran away in fear
in the space between where his ears should have been
a hundred conversations start and begin, he gnashed his teeth
hidden beneath the skin that only protrude when he feeds
he strips off his suit, laying naked in his bed covered in the ash
of the world he knew was already dead

– Ri McCaba

Creative Evolution

The crater may be a natural formation.

The ship is hidden among the fragments of the third moon.

Sometimes the offspring are fertile.

The special children are hidden.

Two thousand kilometers and 120 Kelvin separate them.

They have begun hating each other again.

The mountains: impassable until a future age.

The children still believe in the invisible.

Education is whatever is taught—and inferred.

Magic is whatever they don't understand.

Any predator can move between continents.

Their predecessors sleep in the ice.

No one alive has ever seen the opposite shore.

If there is one.

– F. J. Bergmann

Something in the Air

Few ever notice me, adrift in aether,

beneath the chandeliers of a failing store.

A deformed child, his slack mouth drooling fruit

onto a trendy sweatshirt, howls and clutches

at his caregiver, as our escalators cross,

who startles at the shaking knot of noise.

She sees an empty stage: only bit-part clerks,

who rotate through displays of summer stock.

She checks her sad list: "breakfast cereal, something

he might like." I float down, spin through revolving

doors into the night, become a single unit

of a dazzled host whose yammer circles

buzzing neon. Most agree in principle

with light, but make a covenant with darkness.

– F. J. Bergmann

The Spell

Sleep on, and never wake again.
—The Thousand and One Nights

The enchanted princess sleeps on

inside the crown of long thorns.

She will wake to the sound of a needle

scratching at the end of a vinyl record

when the air turns cool and violet

as Impressionist shadows

and wonder where the years went

without her. In the bed beside her

is a hollow impression of absence.

She will meet her lost ages again

someday, the ghosts of unopened roses.

They will all run into each other by chance

in a Starbucks in an indifferent city,

on the cusp of Accretion & Vying Streets,

as if a random-number generator

were to begin clicking out a string of

infinitely repeating digits, her favorite

lottery numbers, wishes fulfilled,

and they'll fill her in on what she missed,

is still missing, and misses most of all,

like the engine of a truck

she swore she'd checked the oil in

but forgot, as it begins to glow

red-hot, still ticking over

with an occasional grinding noise,

then a tortured, metallic scream,

then the thumbprint of silence.

– F. J. Bergmann

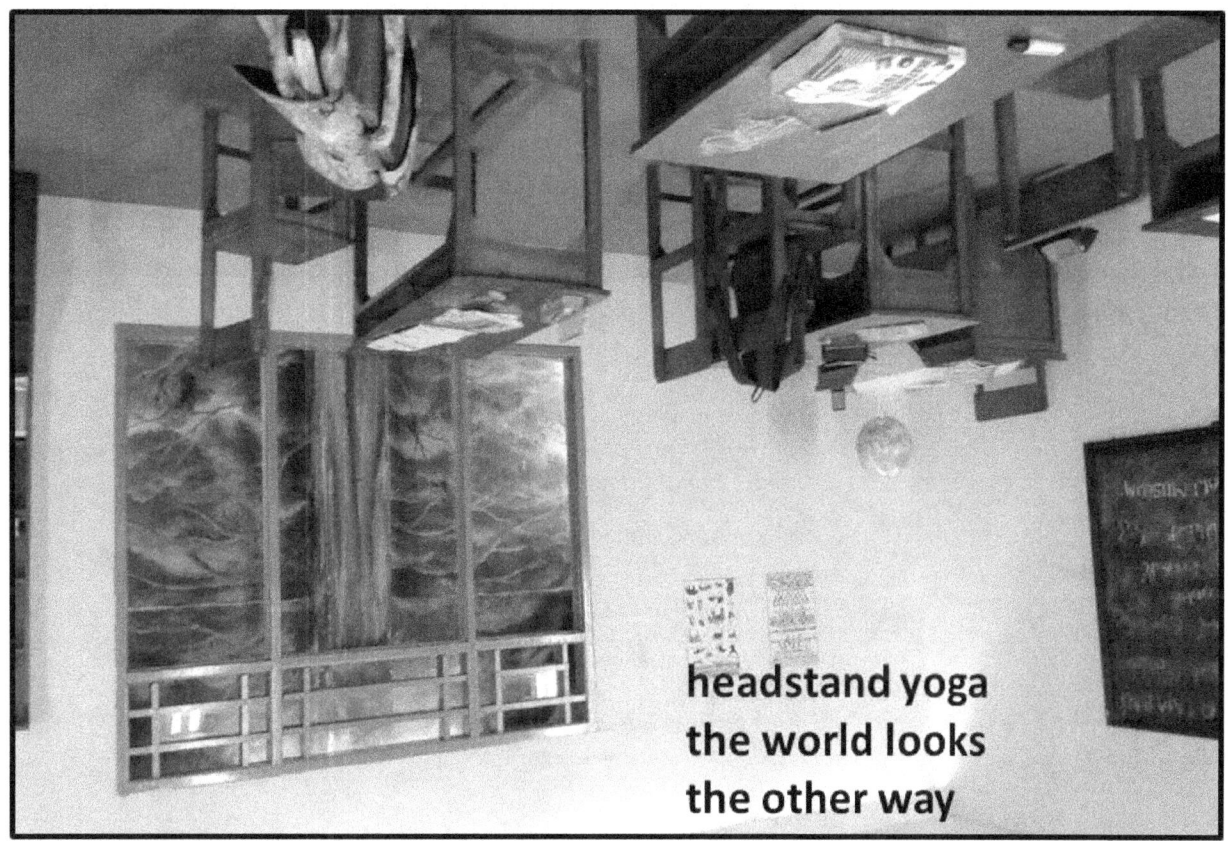

headstand yoga
the world looks
the other way

Photo : 3D Art Museum, Bali & Haiku by Pravat Kumar Padhy

– Pravat Kumar Padhy

the speed
at which i see
the dead coyote

rereading her letter...
I turn the radio volume
down

x amount of time
the dream
i was here

– Tom Clausen

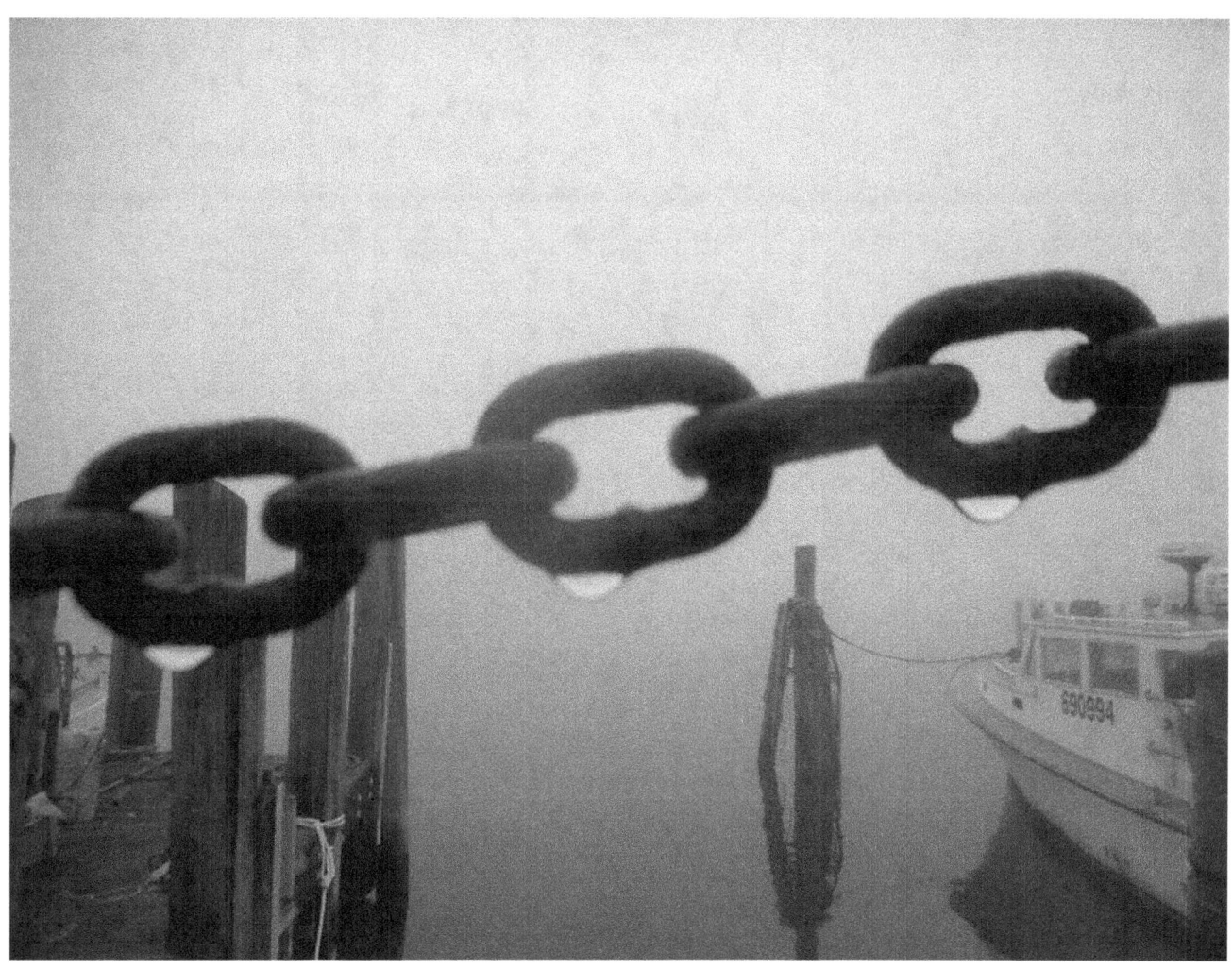

Chain Dripping a Thick Fog

– Tom Clausen

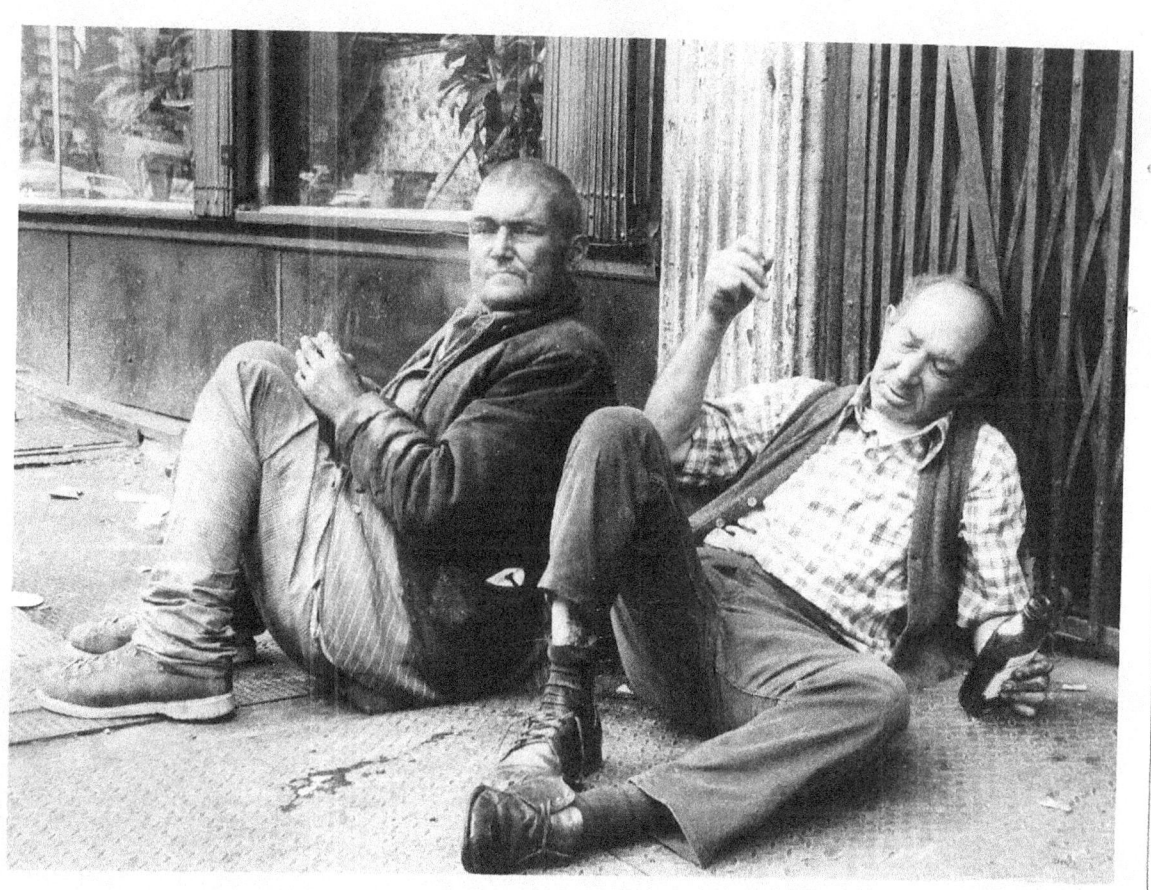

Bowery. N.Y.C 1978

– Tom Clausen

Dust Dance

How great
those gray threads
and new steps -- turning,
as in clouds,
with nothing to cast off,
nothing to begin.
And you want it this way
and it doesn't matter,
and I want it my way,
and I am all antimatter.
I can take form
anywhere.
I can take in the light.
I can take in every moon, every
cloud, in the strand of long fingers
that I am and will be.

– Meg Smith

The First Snow

What more
can I give you --
flashes of cardinals,
sparks that dazzle
out of night.
We could wake
in an Arctic drift,
as though born;
feathers
alight, fleeting.
This is the beginning
but it is done,
as we are.
You must go forward now,
into your
polar night.

– Meg Smith

Emerald Doll

A true thing,
a friend,
in a glossy black dress
with eyes of the light
of sleety stars.
No spoken spell,
no shattered broom,
for none mark the lintel
or portal for us.
There is just us,
you and I
and some cauldron of air.
You and I in our
purple stockings,
holding a light
in our clasped hands.

– Meg Smith

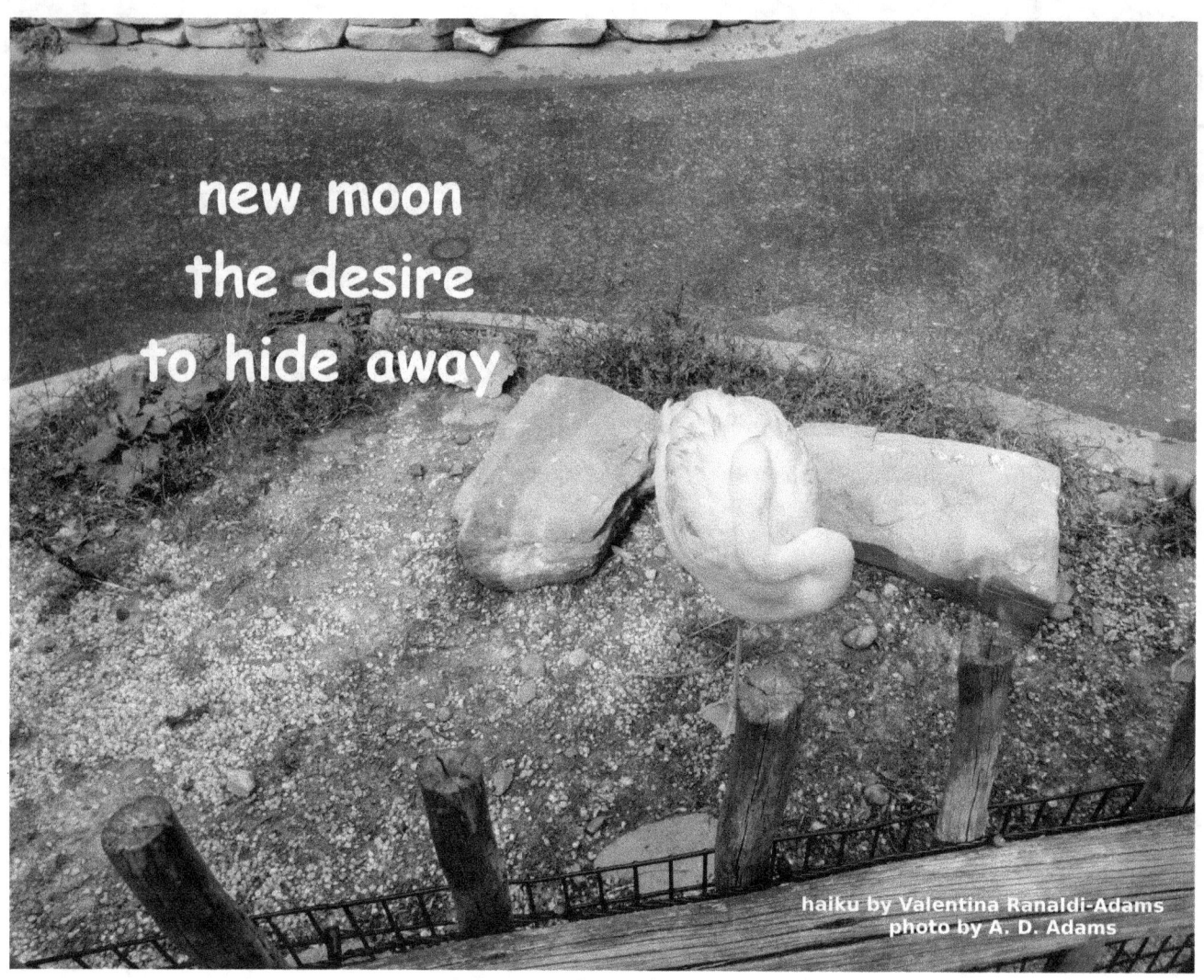

new moon
the desire
to hide away

haiku by Valentina Ranaldi-Adams
photo by A. D. Adams

– haiku: Valentina Ranaldi-Adams, photo: A. D. Adams

Masked Devil

A masked devil
visited me last night
and whispered

come to the class room
I'll show you
banters, cat calls

come to the bank
at the corner of the street
we'll ridicule broken vaults

come to neighbors' garage
we'll stitch the abandoned
skirt of his daughter

– *Aneek Chatterjee*

Reminiscence

I know the person
I'm following; know
the hotel he will visit
know his wine, pale yellow

His girlfriend will now kiss him
and put her hand straight into
his pocket, touch his genitals
and bring out dollars

She'll leave, and the man will
telephone someone to
fix an appointment, take a bath
and go out; -- with his gun

He will cross tramlines, pubs
and a theater, a school
He will enter a by-lane
I know very well …

and shoot me

– *Aneek Chatterjee*

I

The world is not round
the world is
a square with little windows
with a thin curtain
without a door
and inside

me
and
you
are looking for
with blindfolded eyes
the cracks
on the other

II

He
teaches her

to keep
the beauty of love.
She already knows how -
stuffing butterflies
in her stomach

III

Ill-nourished and sleepy
are my words
for you.
I put on flash by your lack
you find your dream
in my absences

– *Radostina A. Dragostinova*

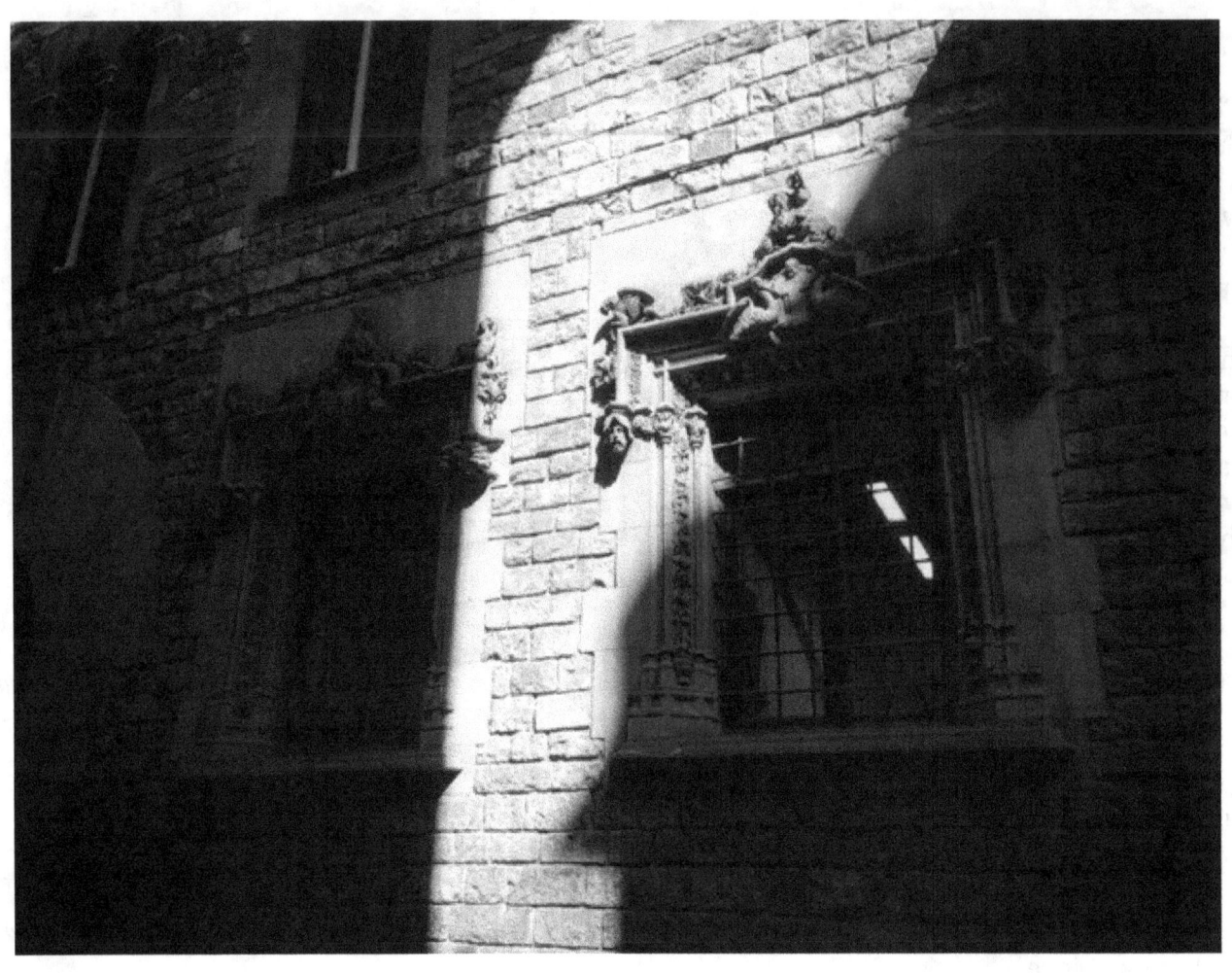

– Radostina A. Dragostinova

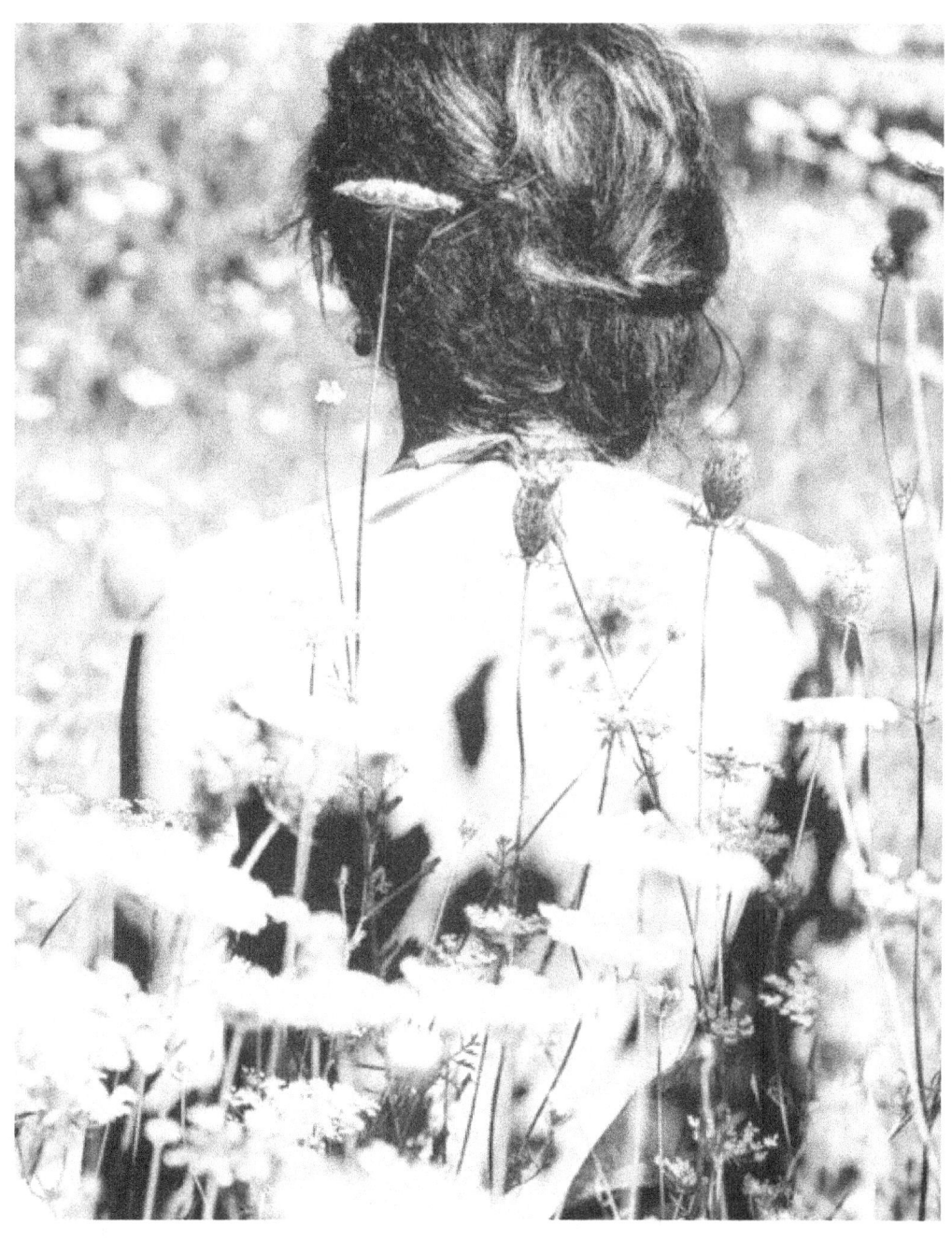

– Radostina A. Dragostinova

–
Radostina
A.

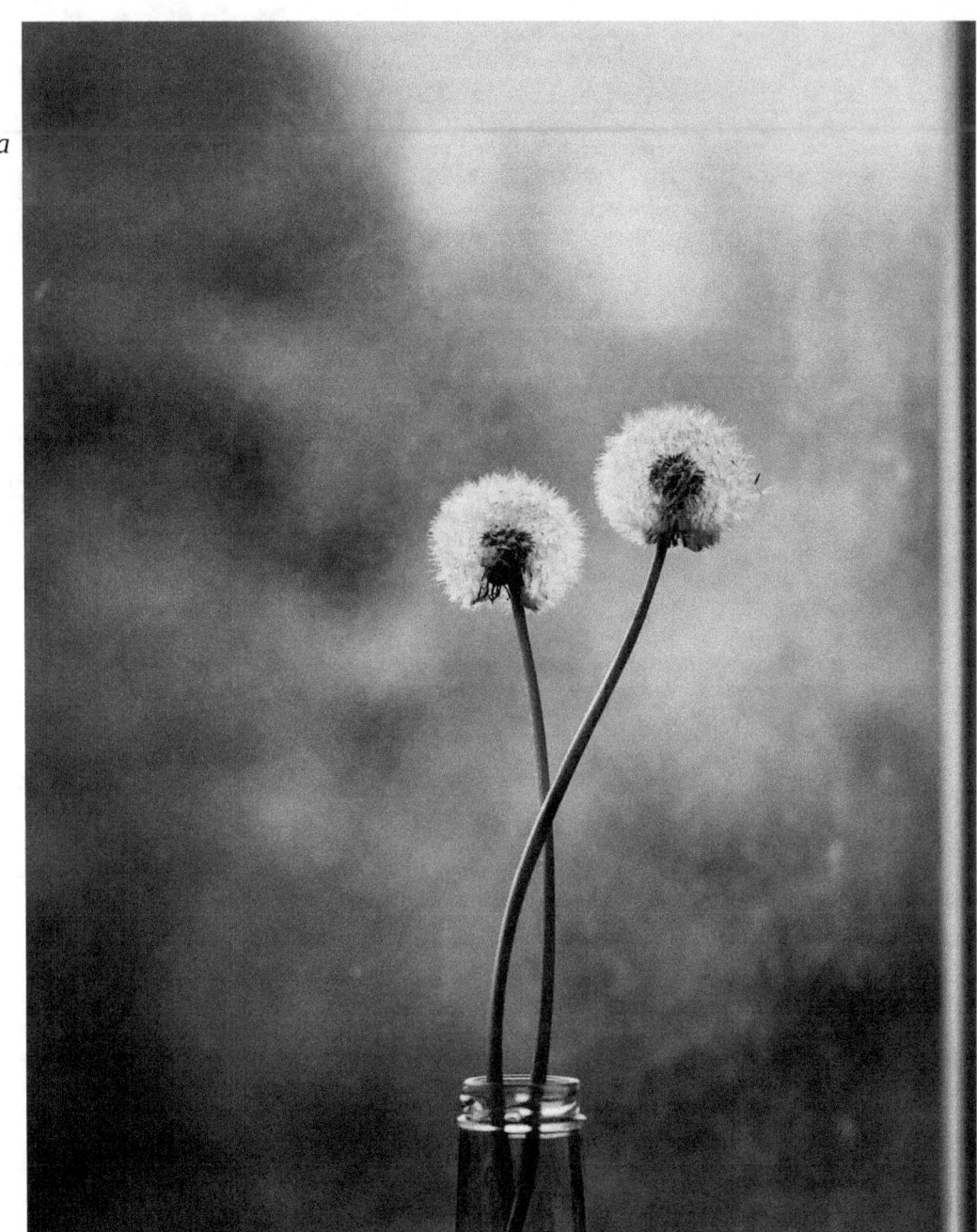

Dragostinova

Lone Wolf

even in the womb
confined by the sac
submerged in saline and blood
I knew my task

beside brothers
birth-right pulsing
fangs bared
at the breast and steaming kill
for my place to gorge

I howl beneath glimmer fields
eyes smouldering among tree hulks
hounding stag and ram
in places of rock and sand
thorn and thistle

I skulk in dark places
alleyways

street-walkers on display
an unwary child
the beggar's boy
I find them

in morning shadows
all is silent
metallic-tang tingles
on my tongue

– Marilyn Humbert

Shingle Beach

surge batters
cliffs to rocks to sand
along the limestone coast

lone shag dives for whiting
black eyed, slick with silver
slippery as soap

sand slips
beneath rubber soles
on the steepest dune

brown snake slithers
to a patch of sun –
languorous light

I'm not afraid
reaching for a trace of you
tears the shadowland veil

we wander
on broken shells and pebbles
among driftwood piles

that day you walked
into the emerald sea
to live entangled
with seagrass

– Marilyn Humbert

the boy with stars for eyes

shadows grow longer on my walk down to the creek. it's time to begin the search beneath the willow's weeping leafy-wands, between the exposed roots gripping the steep bank. dusk is painting the sky orange. light is fading. the stream's water lies glassy-still. a boy, about ten years old rises for air. head tilted back, mouth opens in a perfect circle of pink lips. he breathes in deeply making no sound. his black hair floats cloak-like about his shoulders. I slip further down the bank stretching towards him, to help him from the water. he ignores me. his eyes gleaming stars as he sinks beneath the surface.

recurring dream
glosses ripples
dusk to dawn

– *Marilyn Humbert*

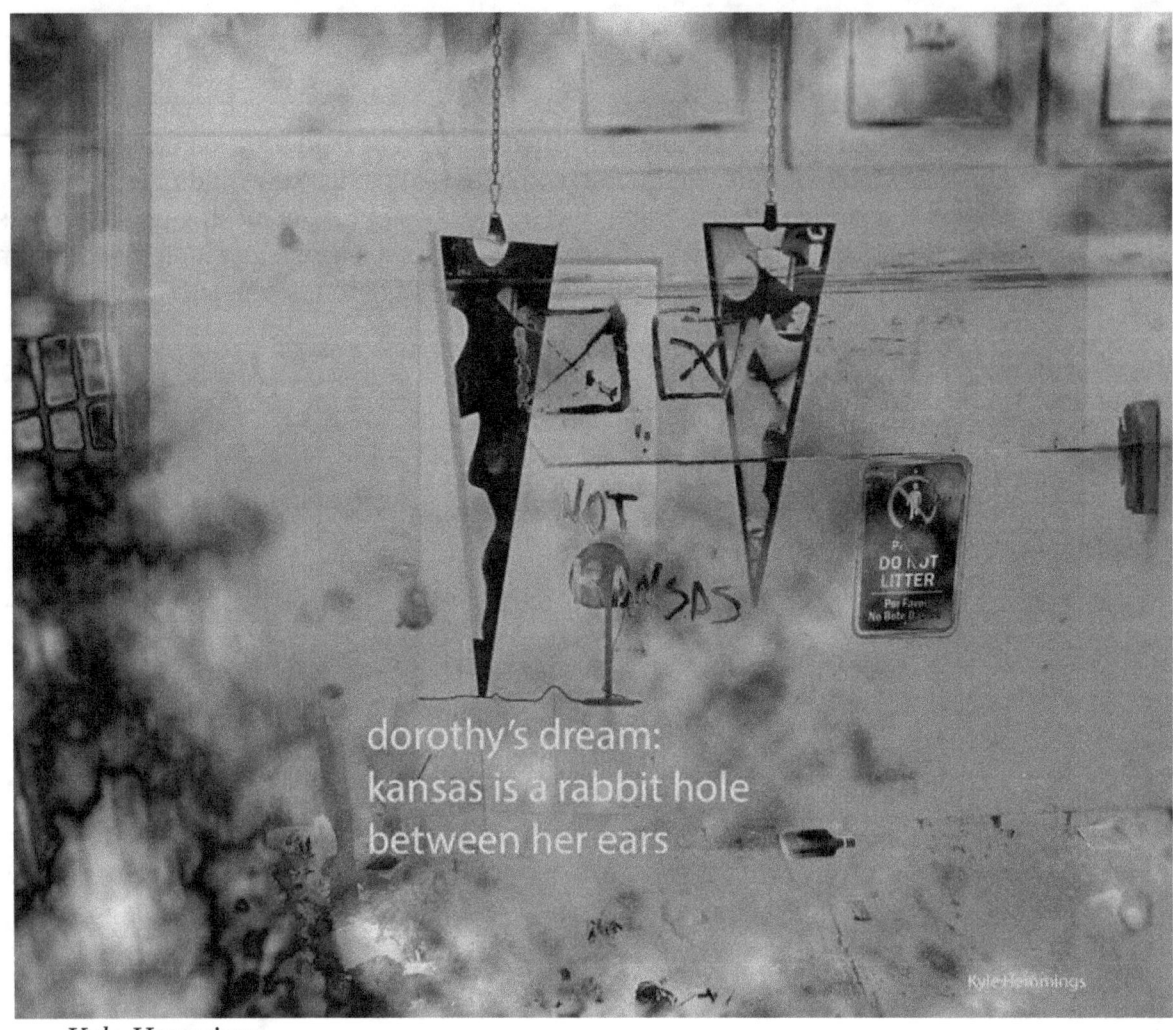

dorothy's dream:
kansas is a rabbit hole
between her ears

– *Kyle Hemmings*

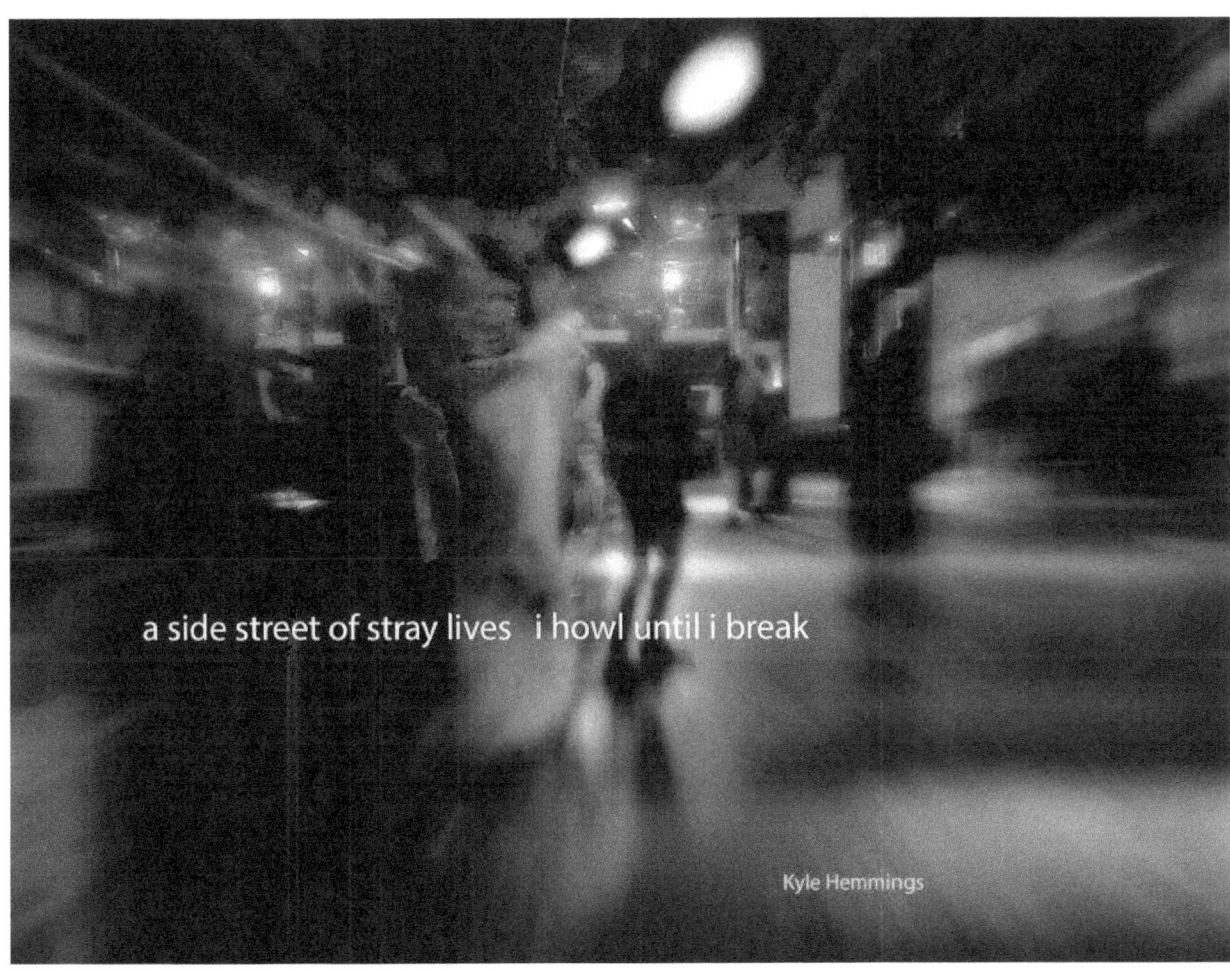

a side street of stray lives   i howl until i break

Kyle Hemmings

– Kyle Hemmings

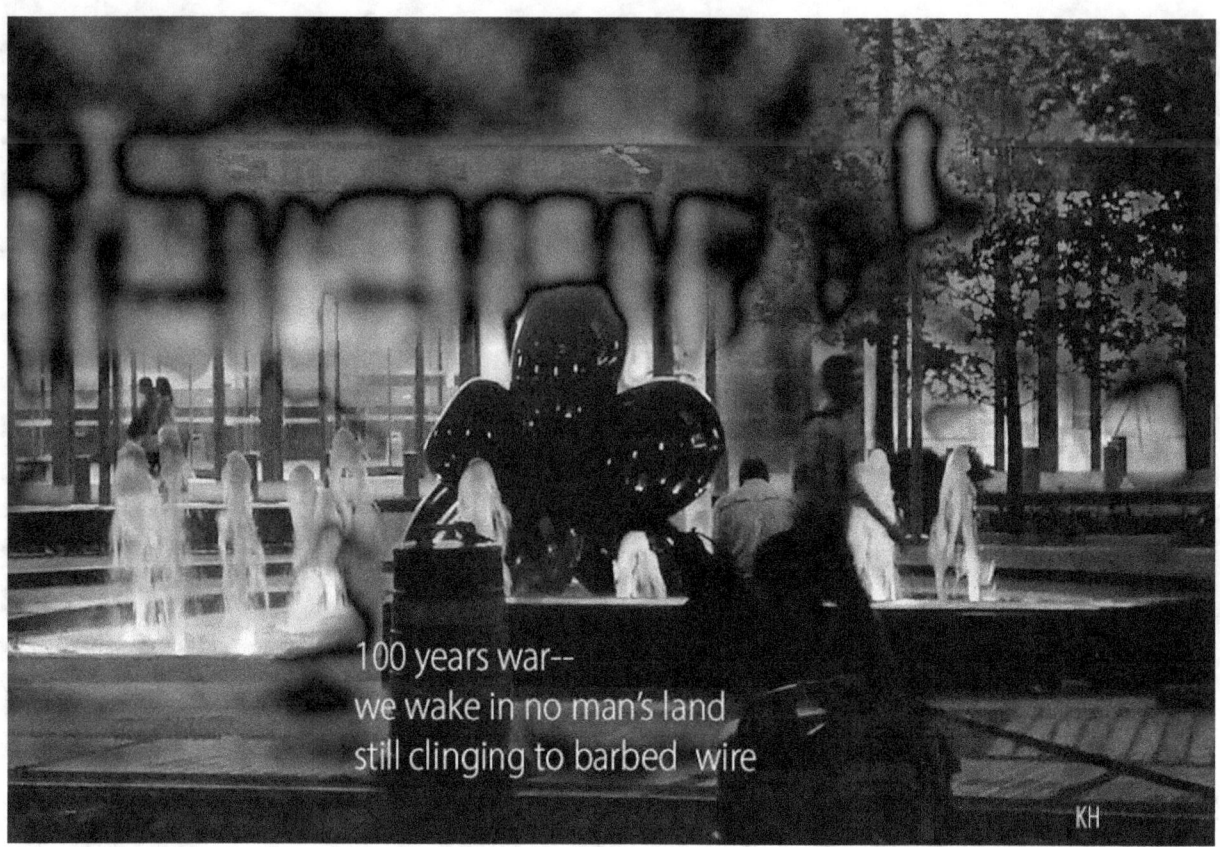

100 years war--
we wake in no man's land
still clinging to barbed wire

KH

– Kyle Hemmings

Relapse

From the dark recesses of my mind,
I give you the pieces,
Of my shattered soul,
Spilled out onto a blank page,
My words, are like a brush,
Painting my pain,
On a blank canvas,
But this time it's different,
This brush has an edge,
With every stroke,
It's painful,
Yet numbing,
I've been here before,
I know the feeling all too well,
A cathartic release,
I'm ashamed it came to this again,
Told myself I wouldn't,
Told myself it would be the last time,
I wish I was stronger…

– _shatteredsoul

Numb

The days are indistinguishable, blurred into one,
I look down at my phone, and it's only Tuesday,
Somehow the length of four days have merged into one,
People say I look 'sad,' that I should be 'happy'
'Cheer up,' they say,
'Look on the bright side,' they say,
But I guess ignorance really is bliss,
Seems like everyone else is moving along with their busy schedules,
Me? I've just been lying here, trying to get myself to finally get out of bed for the past forty-five minutes,
Because if they only knew What really goes on inside my head,
They wouldn't say things like this,
They tell me to try to be happy,
Stop being so sad,
It's funny,
Wish I could scream and cry and throw things,
But I've been staring at the ceiling for the past twenty minutes,
Yes, I wish I was in pain,
Yes, I wish I could cry,
But I can't,
Because right now,
I just feel numb…

– _shatteredsoul

hospice ward the moon slips behind clouds

acid drops sky
he fastens the neck chain
about her throat

winter wedding
her bouquet falls
between gravestones

crematorium
the subtleties of colour
in ash and snow

– John Hawkhead

climbing the ice road   to sober

– *John Hawkhead*

Holiday

Even Death needs to take a break sometime.
Needs to sit on the beach in the sun
with his scythe hidden,
so as not to frighten the swimmers.
Well,
everything about Death has to be hidden.
There can be no exposure
beyond a few inches of face and hands,
hardly more than a woman in a burka.
Yes,
everything has to be hidden,
so as not to frighten the swimmers
ready
for when the holiday is over.

– *Lynn White*

DIRT

I've been tossing and turning and talking in my sleep
Restless reckless wrecked
I spend my days silencing the creatures inside my head
Screaming over the noise of my demons
And the taunting of my skeletons
Wrestling each one as I pull duct tape off a roll and plaster another piece over it's mouth
I bind these ropes tighter and tighter hoping to stop their claws from filleting me from the inside out
The littlest one sits on my nightstand whenever I sleep
His face split open from ear to ear in a smiling grimice of pain and sharp teeth, his skin charred and the color of blood, his eyes black holes that suck me into their gravity
He never says a word but takes joy in reminding me that, even now, I am never alone
I always heard things when I was a kid
Voices
Sounds
Things that weren't there
'Active imagination'
'Seeking attention'
I have been depressed, anxious, bipolar, borderline, defiant, possibly autistic, sensory disordered
Schizoaffective
I hear music in every room of mind, behind every closed door, under the carpets, in between my fingers, stuck in my teeth
Music is the dirt under my nails
Always there
Announcing to the world that I am too sad to take a shower this week, next week, next month
It means I see shadows out of the corner of my eyes that take the shape of aggressive men
I break my neck looking over my shoulder
It means that there are days when I am not enough
The pills are not enough
So I drink from a brown bottle wrapped in my shame
It's the thing I tell on my 3rd or 4th or 5th date to close the door and watch them run
I've always liked the view from back here
It means sometimes my freckles turn into bugs and even they run from me
Sometimes I forget where I am
It's a passionate embrace of words on a page
Even though I am totally alone
And also never alone
I can create a sense of silence
I can hide under a blanket of 26 letters
Sharper than any knife at my wrist
Smarter than any bottle of pills can be
Realer than the demons
Who sit in the shadows
And hide in my mind

– *Kayleigh Wirges*

STITCHES

I woke up tired today
And yesterday
The day before
The kind of tired that's a cross between a sleeping pill
And actually dying
See. I'm so full of words
It's making me drag my feet
Hundreds and thousands and millions of words
But not one that says
I love you so much I hate you
We sit in crowded corners
We hold hands on dark stairs
We gorge ourselves on melancholy
Until we're bloated with memories
And drunken on the past
But we're driving nowhere
Each time I see you I rip my chest open wide
Holding out my heart and my lies and truths and smiles and desires
Dripping with earnest hope and raw innocence
Coated in black sticky fear
And I remember who I am
Who you are
And who we are not
As I stuff each part of me back into my ribs and
Stuttering
Shaking
Sloppy
Stitch my skin back into place
Taming my expectations
And as the tired old lion lies down
Sated with this scrap of meat
I hold my rattled breath knowing
This is not my last fight
I have earned the blood on my teeth

– *Kayleigh Wirges*

SHOCK

Maybe you've heard of
Electric convulsive therapy
Shock therapy
It leaves tinder spots on my forehead
Like sunburn
It leaves a bruise
Or two
Or three
On my arms and hands
It takes with it my memories
And
The sadness
That creates paintings and words
It takes passion and replaces it with quiet apathy
The sadness that has been my companion
Since I was 6 or 7
Sadness- the thing I know best in the world
No
Not sadness but despair
I exist in existential crisis and
Electric conclusive therapy
Dims the road out of view
It takes away all the off ramps
And puts me in the middle of the freeway
Safe from harm
But alone in the world
Without even sadness
To hold in my chest

– Kayleigh Wirges

It's Raining Dead Birds

Maybe they were cooked alive by the heat?
The blazing sun's been ever present lately,
the dry, northern wind blows through the mountains
where no one has seen dew or snow for ages.

In the azure sky turning lavender one sees
indigo rays like laser beams,
shooting stars or sharp sparkles –
they were supposed to be four on horseback –

not iridescent signs alighting the heavens,
evenly scaring people all around the globe.
Lava splendor, inescapable torpor, dog days;
the apocalypse never said it would rain dead birds.

– *Walter Ruhlmann*

Road 6009

Through the vineyards, down the hills,
the wind mills eyeing you,
you drive this pale, yellow car
he bought when you dwelt in the mountains.

Now this land of rocks and dust, grapes and reeds,
whipped by the northern wind, dried by the sun.
Some women stand on the side, hustle,
old wine makers, Spanish drivers stop by.

You drive on this road to go to work –
though you commute by train most of the time.
Trucks, tourists, dangerous bends,
drive you to choose safety.

In case your need to disappear,
to leave this place but leave no trace,
your tiredness or your death wish,
made your car crash into some tree.

– *Walter Ruhlmann*

Whorehouse

I spent so many nights fucking,
sucking erected cocks,
caressing lifeless skins, grey hair,
deadly Indians.

Ungrateful pale moons touched the bottoms of the lakes
where the bloody tadpoles mewled endlessly.
On the banks, the nymphs parted their thighs
greeting the destitute phalluses of the old.

A limitless hotel,
the blue sky as the only frontier,
the ground is below,
all around hundreds of erected dicks.

And I waited for my turn,
my ass trained to please,
spread on a polyester bed
as on a ship pitching on the enraged seas.

– Walter Ruhlmann

I sleep on my back
late late afternoon
in the old house
beneath the tiled roof
suddenly feel
a pinch—
lost child, a ghost, or something
intent on awakening me

there's the moon
full, blurred, drifting
in and out of black shadows
the race across
snowy mountains
the Sea of Japan

earlier in the day
you stood
at the edge
of the road, rice fields
photographing mist
beneath an
orange umbrella

you are
the only child
I'll ever have,
now grown
to woman
you smile
that full smile
from both corners
of your mouth

– *Miriam Sagan*

sealskin coat
the tides within
pulling pulling

fallen tree
twisted branches
fashion a crow

shadows
between the rain tremor
fibromyalgia

thistledown
her collection jar
fills with dreams

molten silver
the moon grows
another hare

new moon
behind the owl mask
her frightened face

– *Andy McLellan*

AIR

That spring in Kyoto, few people had heard of the word retrovirus or knew what it meant. As the sakura zensen (cherry blossom front) reached the old capital, hanami (blossom picnics) took place as usual. Couples and families gathered beneath the trees, spreading out their blankets to share food and sake as they have done for centuries. Stories and laughter fell from open mouths as the blossom drifted around them.

The first cases seemed little more than an allergic reaction. Patients were admitted to the university hospital with mild breathing difficulties after being in close proximity to flowering trees, but these resolved quickly in the emergency room with the administration of a little oxygen and some reassuring words.

In the days following, a small trickle of patients became a flood, and consultants from the Ear, Nose and Throat department found themselves being called to the ER with increasing regularity. More and more patients were admitted for overnight stays to stabilise their breathing, and a general warning was released to the population of the city that cherry blossom viewing was now considered something you should do at your own risk, with breathing masks advised as a caution.

Overnight, Maruyama Park, and other traditional places for hanami became deserted. The rest of Kyoto settled into a sombre silence quite unlike any other spring in recorded memory.

One week after the first signs, 23-year-old Yuko Konomi became patient zero, the first fatality from what was now being called Sakura yamai (Cherry blossom disease). Her parents stood by her bedside as doctors desperately tried to revive her, unwilling to give up while any hope remained. Eventually, even they resigned themselves to the inevitability of such a young death.

As Yuko's face turned white, a single pale pink blossom appeared from between her lips.

No one said a word.

under the old oak
my breath
becomes hers

– Andy McLellan

going over his plan
once again
thief moon

airstrike
the glow
of fireflies

in my twenties
and already bored
with this life
a small brown recluse
spins its web slowly

old blues music
down to the seeds
and stems

– Gabriel Bates

Far from Home

It's a long drive to the art museum. An hour, minus rush hour, to be exact. So, I pass the time repeating some mantras that, according to all of these popular self-help books I read, will greatly benefit my mental health:

I am beautiful.

I am worthy.

I am safe.

Honestly, I am still waiting to see if they work, but in the meantime, I guess they can't hurt.

self-love
I tell myself
what they don't

— Tiffany Shaw-Diaz

Irony

You stole my happy poems
then asked where they went
you unplugged the sun
and wondered how I became so comfortable
in the dark
you taught me consequences do not apply
and somehow my irresponsibility puzzles you
you showed me life is a mixed bag
of pain
and you are terrified of my obsession
with death

– Bekah Steimel

Seeing Red

My father is a nightmare. My mother is a dream. How childish, but abuse and big love keep us rooted as children. My father is Satan, red and shaking a fist at the world. My mother is Santa Claus. She wears a different red. A rose red. My life revolves between the two. Then, suddenly I am covered in the confusing color, neck to ankle. My father is a bull now, twenty deadly paces away. Head lowered and eyes wild, he stomps his hooves and shakes the world. He only sees me. I am to blame right now. I cannot outrun him. The "Exit" signs flash the angry red, and I know this is a trick. Something worse waits for me on the other side if I try to leave. This is his twisted kingdom. I close my eyes and brace for the horns and heat of this madness. When I open them, there is my mother, built like a shield of light and flesh. She is not an angel. She is more practical than that. She bursts into a hundred painted clowns. Some lead me to safety, a patch of green grass under the only piece of blue sky, but most circle my father. They dizzy and frustrate him. Rage is exhausting. When his knees hit the ground, the earth trembles once more. And, then it is over. A hundred painted clowns meld back into my mother.

– Bekah Steimel

Cancer Lyric E

I love you. You are dead. Which three words are most relevant today? I've spoken the former, screamed the former, gasped the former. My traumatized lips can barely whisper the latter. But they are just as true, just as pertinent. They matter, even if I cannot declare them. I designed my life around "I love you." Those three tiny words were the nucleus of the cell we shared. Now three other tiny words have placed me in a different cell. Alone. I am serving time for a crime I did not commit. I am neither culprit nor victim, but that does not matter. I am just another casualty of love and death. I love you, and you are dead.

– Bekah Steimel

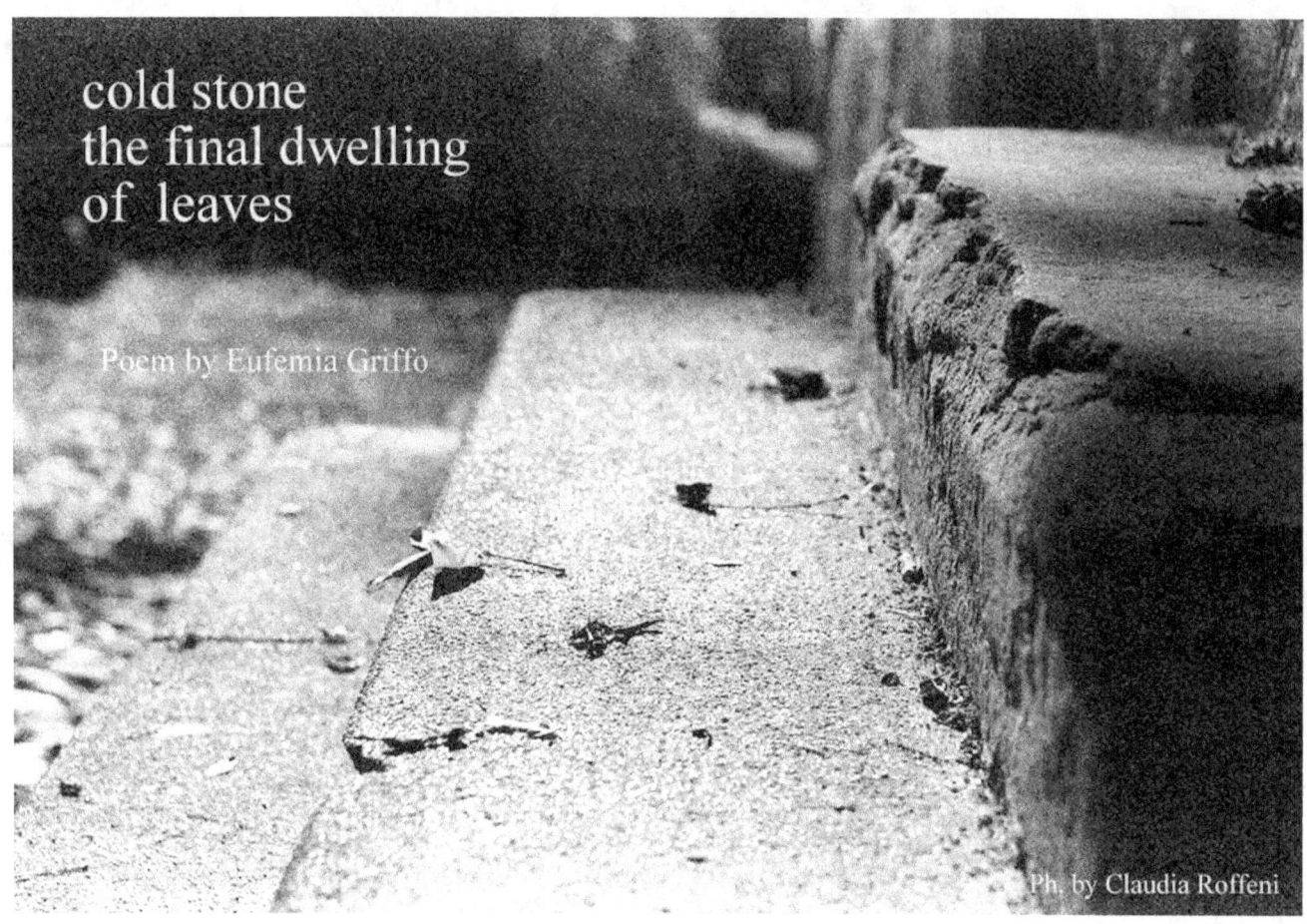

cold stone
the final dwelling
of leaves

Poem by Eufemia Griffo

Ph. by Claudia Roffeni

– Eufemia Griffo

ruined house
clouds take the form
of a dark demon

Poem by Eufemia Griffo

Ph. by Claudia Roffeni

— Eufemia Griffo

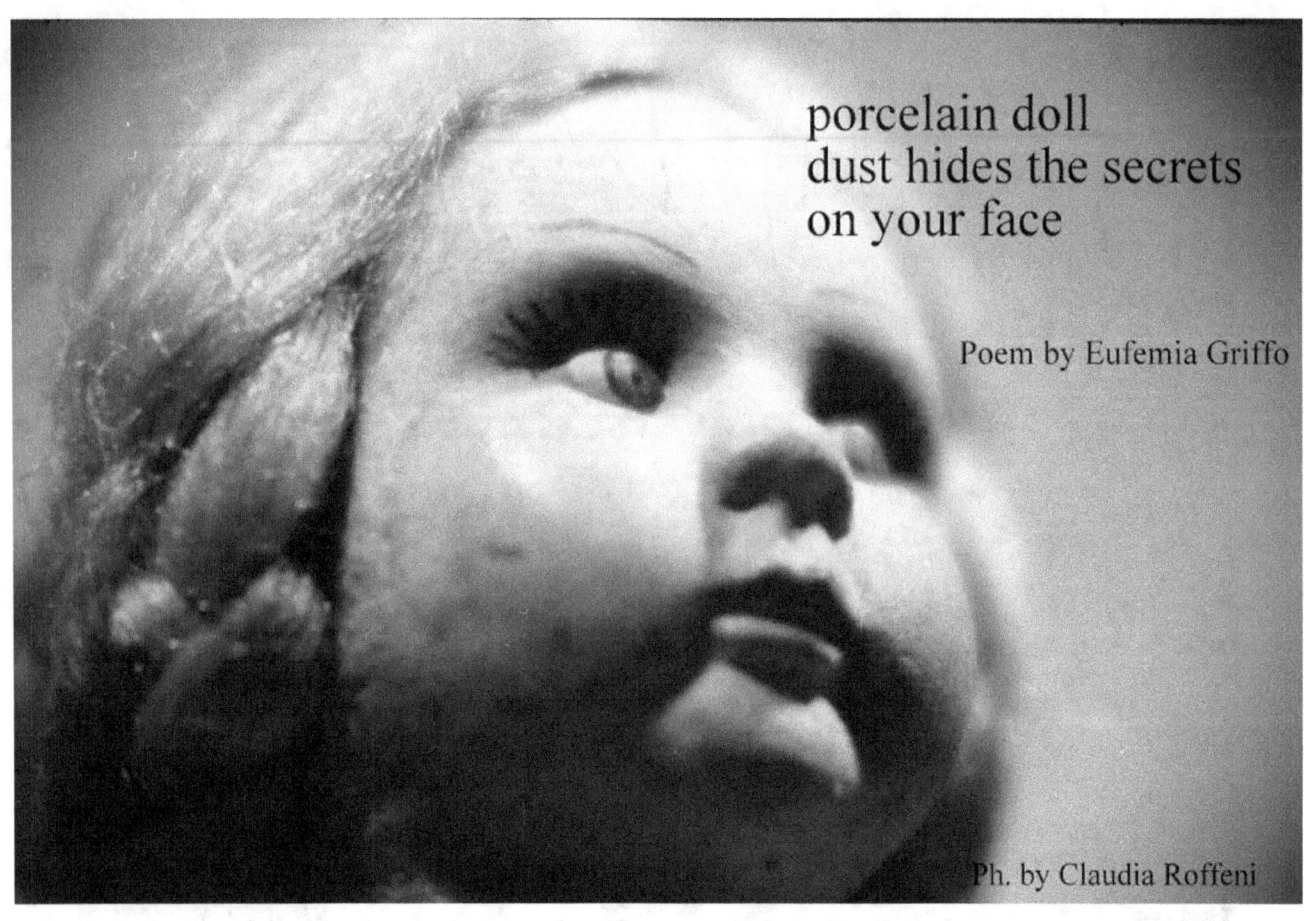

porcelain doll
dust hides the secrets
on your face

Poem by Eufemia Griffo

Ph. by Claudia Roffeni

– Eufemia Griffo

DEADLY JEWELLERY

This curved metal
Gripped until bright
By a soldier's finger
Released the shells
Into the chamber,
Tripped the hammer,
Propelling danger.

Now remoulded
Into a ring
Of attractive design,
It bears a stone
Made of polished lead,
From a case that
Held a bullet head.

Such jewellery
Born of conflict,
Seduces the senses,
Attracts the eyes
And draws in the breath,
For grim fragments
Once fashioned for death.

– David Subacchi

DEAD LEAVES

And so the clearing up of leaves, bored by their shade
A short lived display of yellow that only depressed
We arm ourselves with sharp rakes in faded coats dressed
Like hurried scarecrows an impatient farmer made.
The scraping of steel on ground where paving was laid
The hunting through grass and piercing of soil compressed
Frantically bayonetting as soldiers possessed
No prisoners taken no ransom to be paid.

This annual ritual little comfort brings
With dark winter brooding silently in the wings
And our minds fixated on political things
We challenge each dog that barks and bird that sings.
Piled high with dead foliage fierce bonfires burn
Our hopes spiralling upwards never to return.

– David Subacchi

beside
the tattoo parlor
gravestones

– Gary Eaton

MIDNIGHT GRAVEYARD

As the darkness makes me uncomfortable
I realize they don't care. Light is lost on them.
The awareness strikes me as a sudden blow
filling me with mortifying sadness.
Their sealed, uniform ignorance
has the obscenity of an ill-scarred wound.

How can they see nothing, hear nothing?
Quiet is also their lot. I long
for a hush, murmur, whisper
but no gush of wind graces this stillness.
I had not understood in daytime
how forsaken they are, the extent of oblivion.

They say souls of our departed remain.
Only if recent and close.
All those whom we don't know simply vanish.
In the night I feel the pressure of nothingness
I crave a ghostly breath, a scream
shredded shrouds hanging from naked branches.

Here. A deer steps out of the woods,
crosses my path. As I stop mesmerized
it transfixes me, with a fierce icy stare.
I exult and I shiver. This epiphany cheers me
yet the look of the wild pierces through me
summoning my own expendability.

One day nature will claim back
this wholeness, and reign undisturbed.
I feel both small and redundant.
The departed sleeping underground
are of no comfort. They betray me
as they have been betrayed.

– Toti O'Brien

FEBRUARY

Not because you have died
should I miss the wisteria blooming
or when blossoms of citruses
will explode full force in the backyard
omit to inhale as deep as I can.

I'll remember the vial of lemon essence
you sent when I turned fifty
the last present you gave me.
In your greeting note you called me
'fragrant' and I am grateful.

You have died at the break of dawn
on Saint Valentine day, not a week
away from my birthday, stamping
my beloved month of February
with your mark.

Though you were my brother
only, you have cheated on me.
Cheated cruelly, though you
were my brother only.
In case you'd be tempted to forget.

– Toti O'Brien

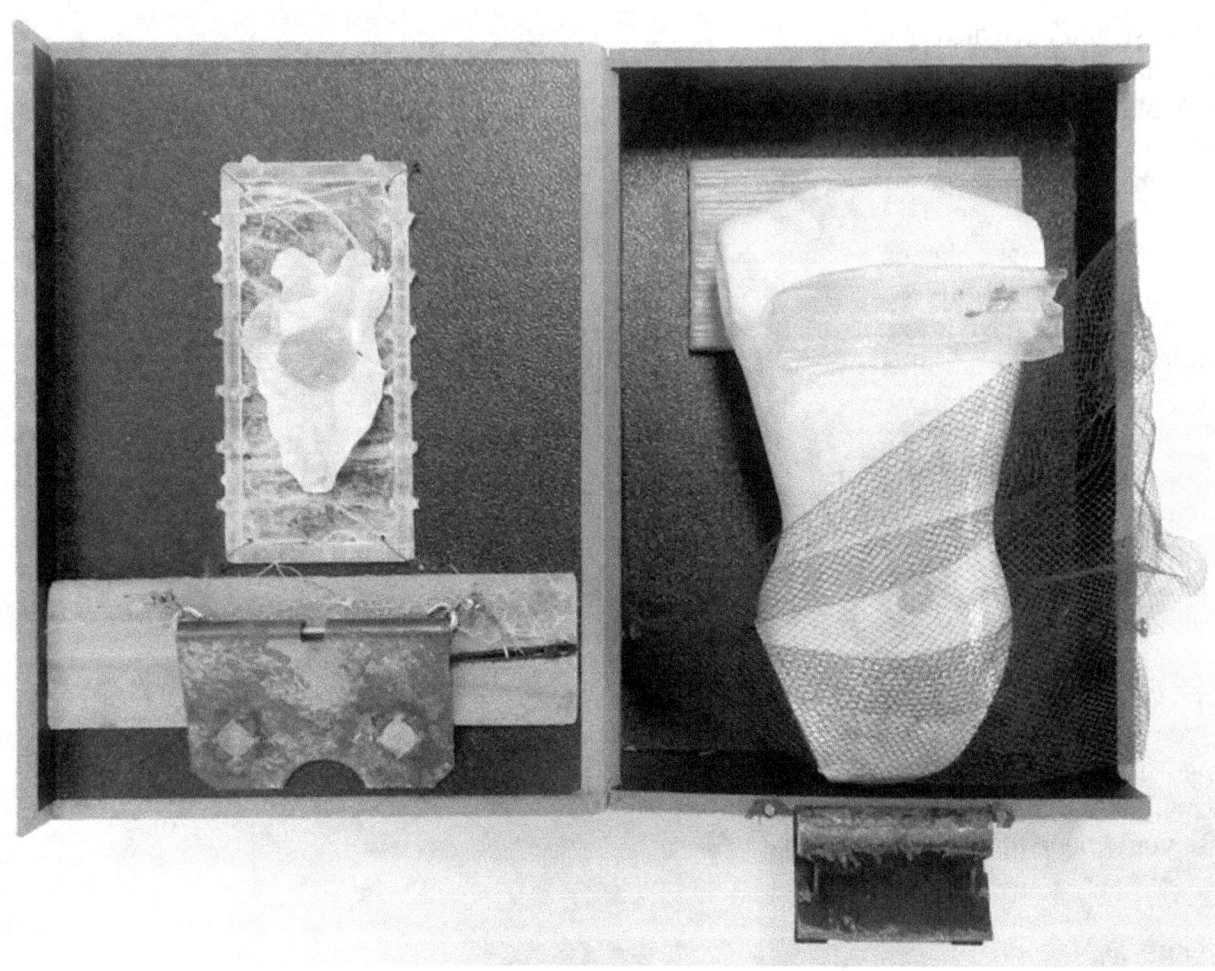

Alchemy 1, Brass

– Toti O'Brien

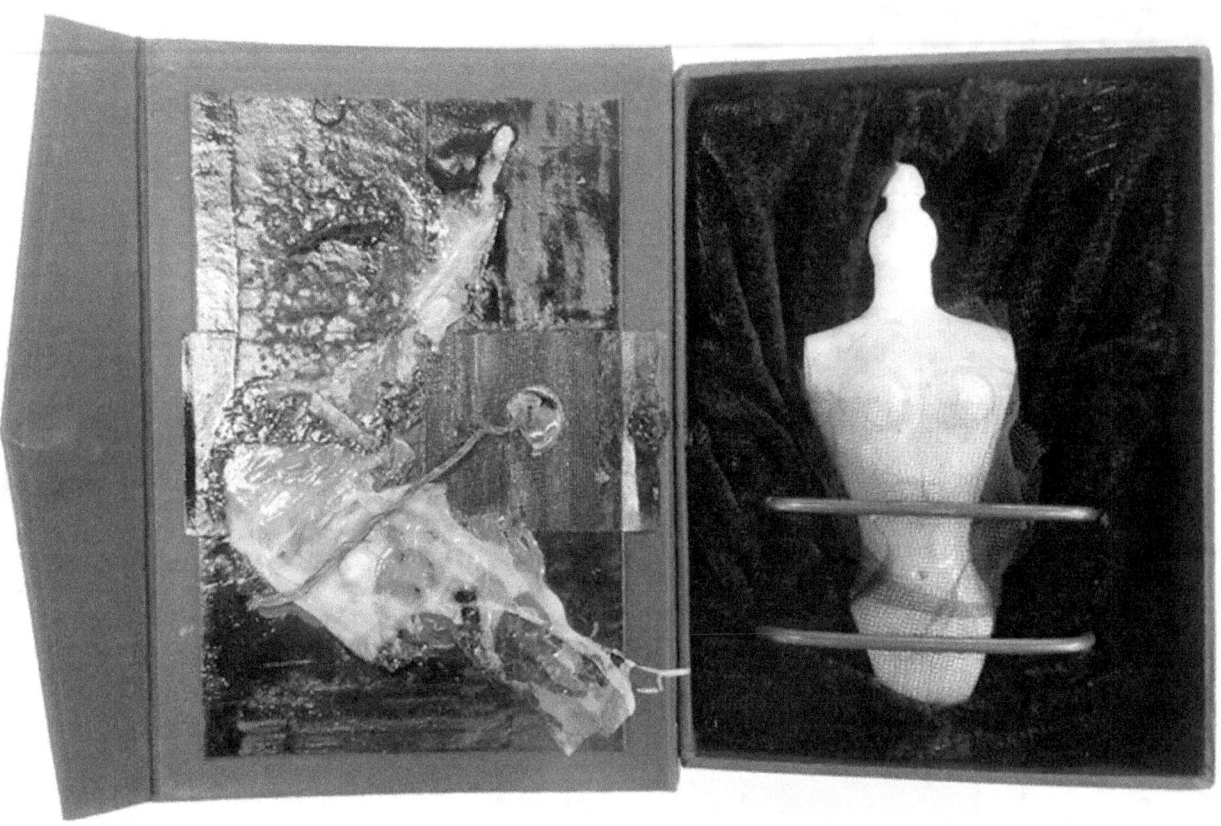

Alchemy 2, Milk

– Toti O'Brien

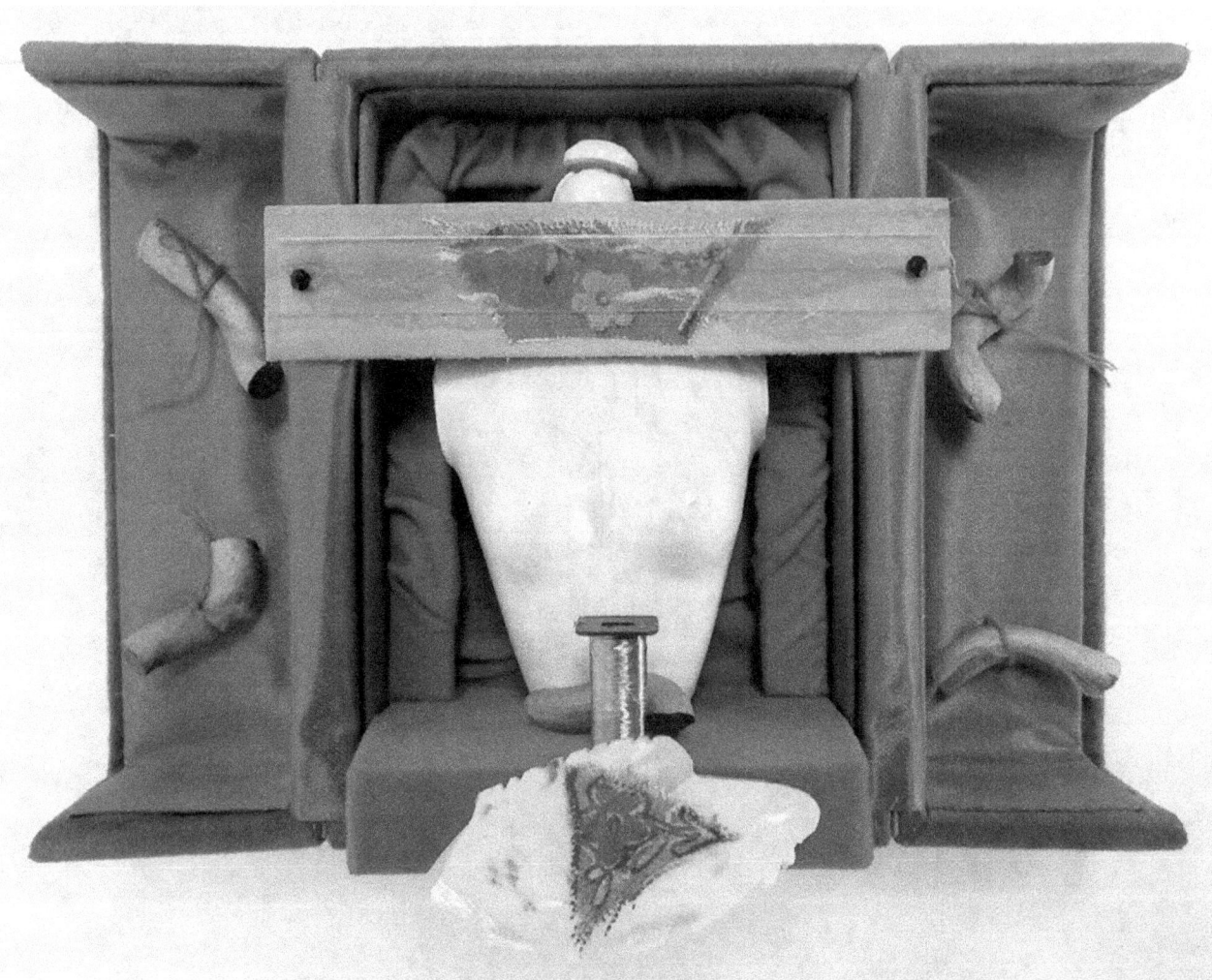

Alchemy 3, Gold

– Toti O'Brien

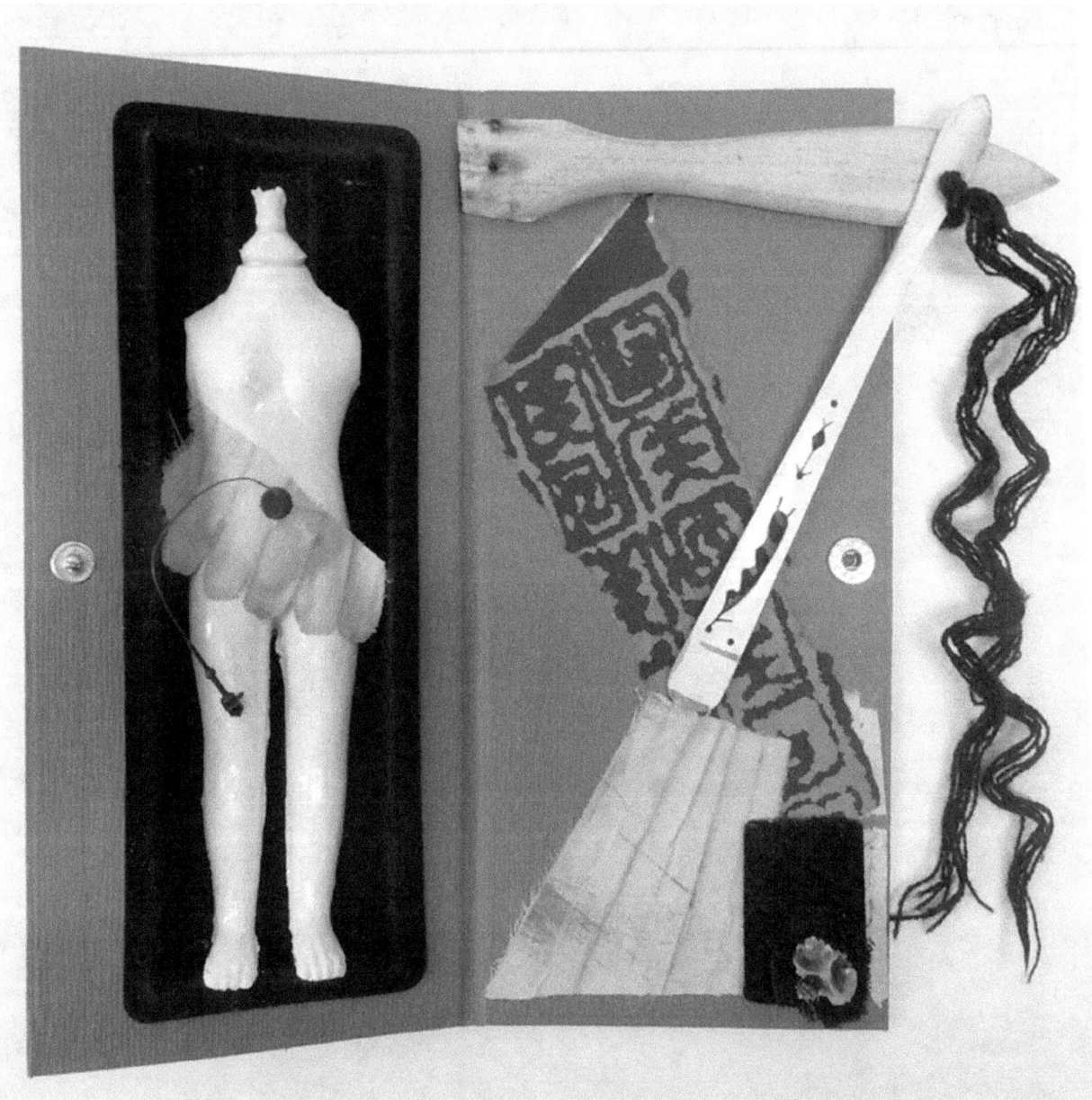

Alchemy 4, Ink

– Toti O'Brien

My Father Made Men

Though he never much went to
school-he taught me lessons
I haven't found the
distance to forget.

Carved into memory
that dawn thunder shook
the morning like a fever
choking me in a grasp
of power too foreign
to understand.

My father's
rifle obliterating
nature's calm without warning.
And the bird that fell silent
bleeding and dead from
the sky was only my
first lesson at age six.

Holding up the destroyed bird
to me-he said, "death, this is
what happens to all of
us."

Scaring me so horribly that
I burst into tears and ran to the cottage.
That night, my father said to my mother-
"maybe it's your fault, I don't know
but it will take longer than I
thought to make him
a man."

– *Rp Verlaine*

After Therapy

She took me home.
It was a lonely place
of books and lies
and both of us
for a scant few hours.

Making love on satin sheets
besmirched by blood, whiskey and undetermined stains.
She was thin with black hair and soft bruised skin.
Her vocabulary limited to vague commands like
"that's it"and "don't stop."

We had met in therapy
community service for me and for her...
well she never spoke. She was like
ice that was far too thin and you could
see the cracks.

Yet her remote distant eyes couldn't be refused
at least not by me. And though that day she
might've settled for anything- the sex was
pleasing enough for her that
when it was over-
she smiled for the first time.
Kissing my ring-less fingers.

For many minutes nothing was said
we lay mute as shadows that had
suddenly found light.

And then she asked me to leave
she was expecting her husband
at any minute, he liked to beat her
and this was her way of
getting even.

– *Rp Verlaine*

everyone dies
why should I read
to the bitter end

stillborn
still named
still   grieving

that little boy
who pulled the petals
from daisies
decided no-one loved him
now he catches flies

– David J Kelly

damp

a light
thunderstorm
erupts

someone actually
pulls over
and offers me
a ride

the drought has finally
passed our city

the rain
fills my fractured
back

and carries me home to an Advil
and the dark algorithm
of YouTube

– Marshall Bood

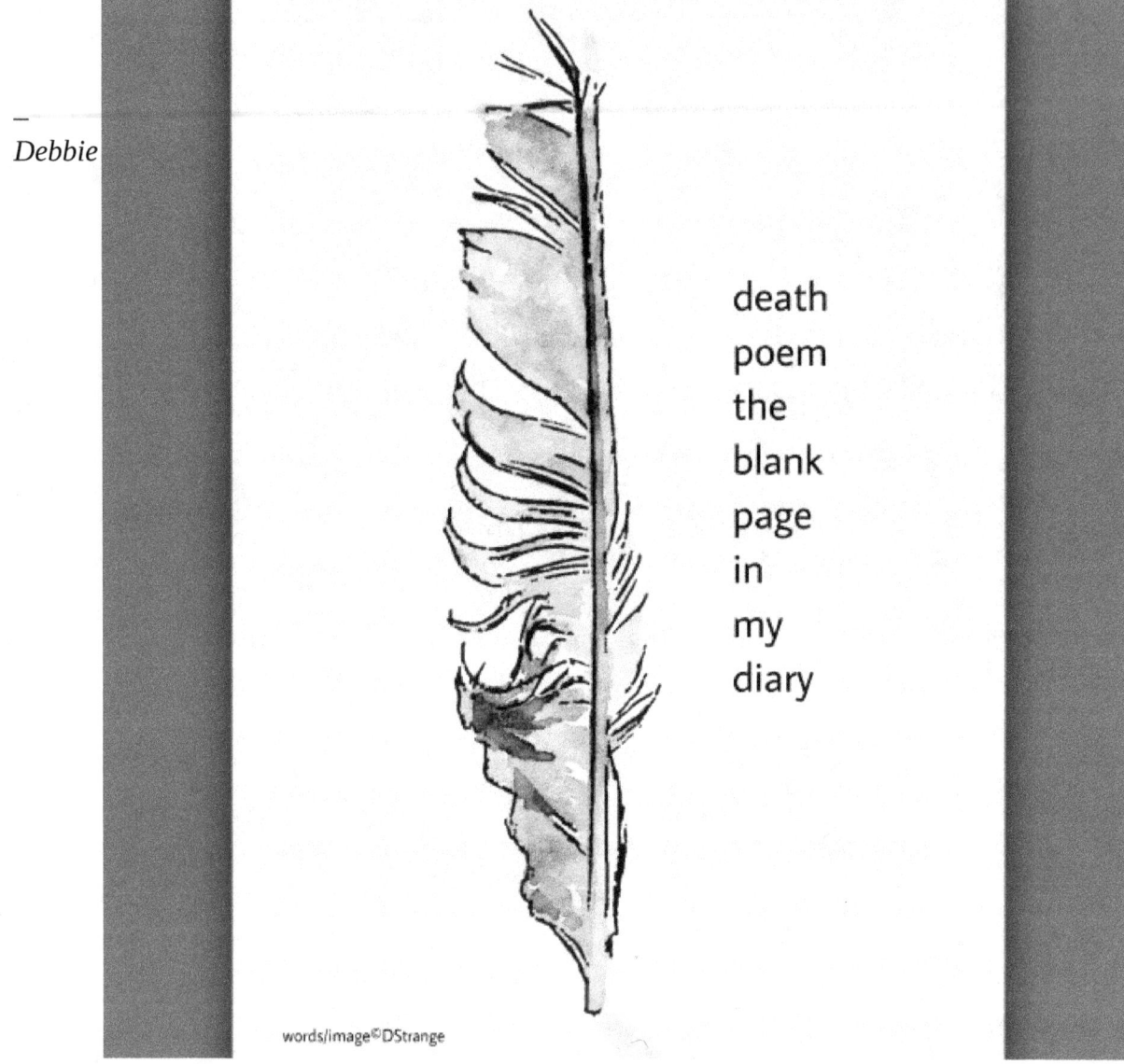

Debbie

Strange

death
poem
the
blank
page
in
my
diary

words/image©DStrange

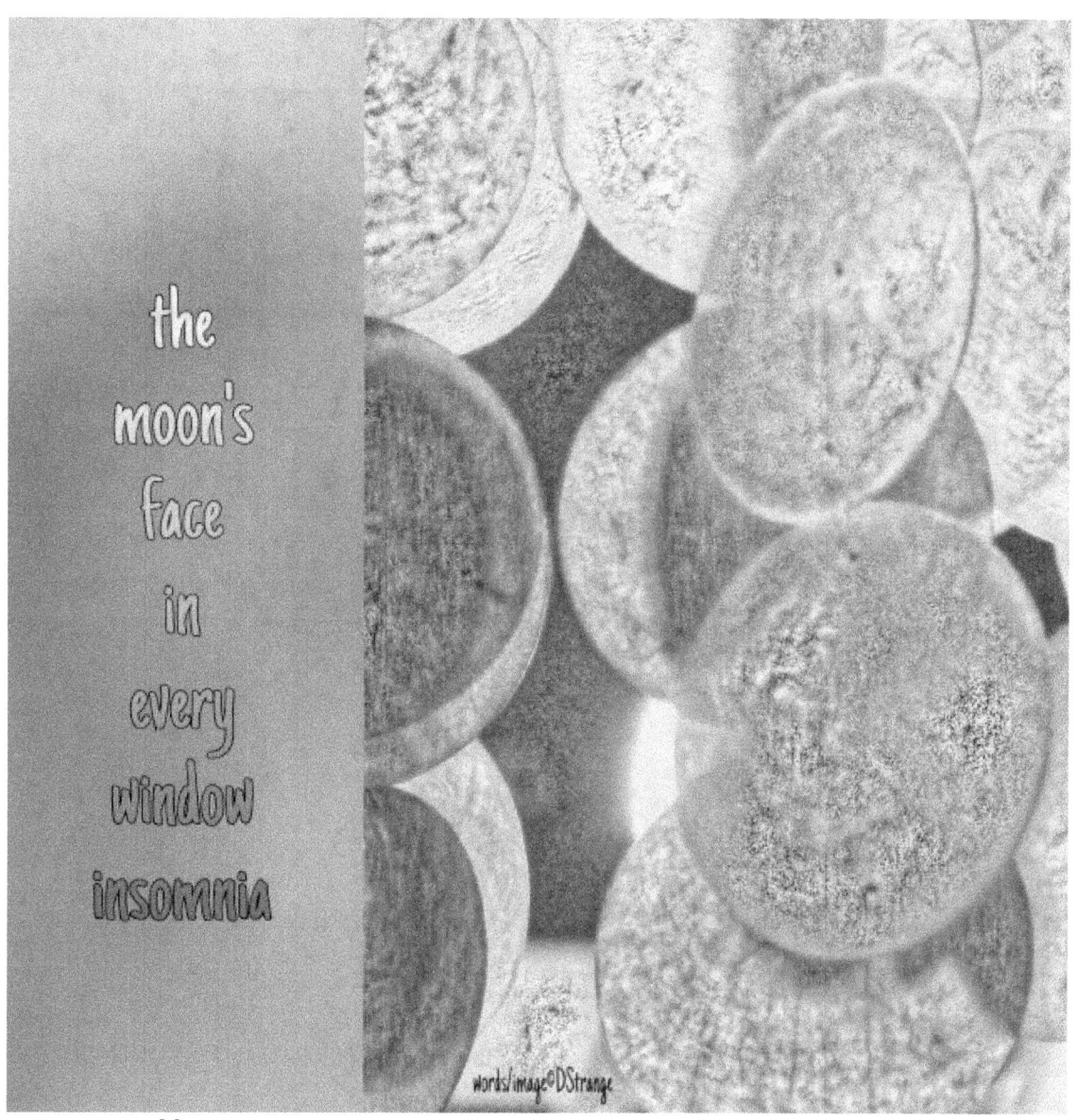

the
moon's
face
in
every
window
insomnia

words/image©DStrange

– *Debbie Strange*

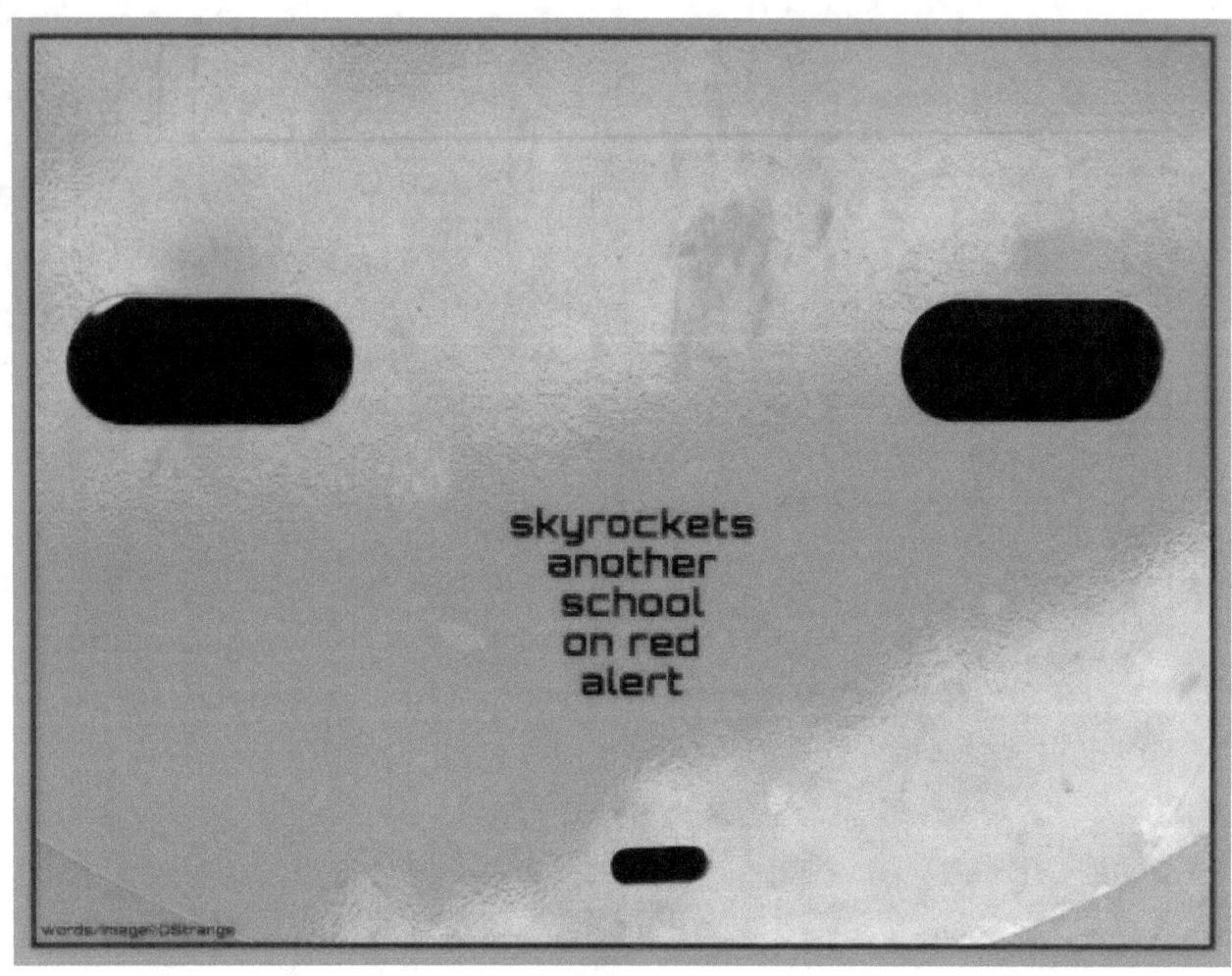

skyrockets
another
school
on red
alert

words/image@DStrange

– *Debbie Strange*

The Monster Under The Bed

Behind closed doors,
the attack inevitable.
Velvet darkness consumes,
the heart a bass line.
His candy cane legs unfold,
the eyes that glow
blink open like a switch.
The spider hands ready themselves,
those Nosferatu claws,
reaching for an ankle to grab.
The fist pops out, a Jack in a Box,
a boxing glove on a spring,
a concussive lullaby –
knocked into next week's sleep.

– *Kirsty A. Niven*

The Knife

I haven't done this in years.
The once scarlet slashes,
those stripes that marked my tabby coat,
have now faded to crinkled moon tissue.
Years have passed, those wounds healed
and now new ones gape open.

The pallid skin sighs under the glint of the knife –
how it has missed its cool embrace.
The jagged mouth parts its lips,
longing to be kissed again,
its lipstick smeared in a waxy smudge
as the blade penetrates, coming home.

The wound, the colour of roses,
of Valentine's gifts that won't arrive;
the colour of poppies,
a bloody battlefield. Eye-popping.
I long for its opium, the numbness
that comes with each slice.

I don't want to come back,
the lives just won't run out –
a torturous cycle, a Sisyphus struggle.
I claw my way back again and again,
all for nothing, no redemption.
The call of the knife is too strong.

– Kirsty A. Niven

Alice

I'm not all there myself,
losing my something, my everything –
vanished in a sea of tears, a pool of pig blood;
an impossible shower of playing cards
that came tumbling forth
from the rabbit hole prematurely,
unravelling like madness.

Lifeless stop motion figures
birth from me, these corpse creatures
a mimsy statistic, 1 in 4,
going out altogether like candles.
I paint the roses red with their blood,
saturating the white
with its congealed muck.

It takes all the running I can do
to keep from falling further,
descending into serpentine riddles
of self pity that eat away at every last smile.
A nonsensical horror,
a Svankmajer twist on the tale –
this wasn't how it was supposed to end.

– *Kirsty A. Niven*

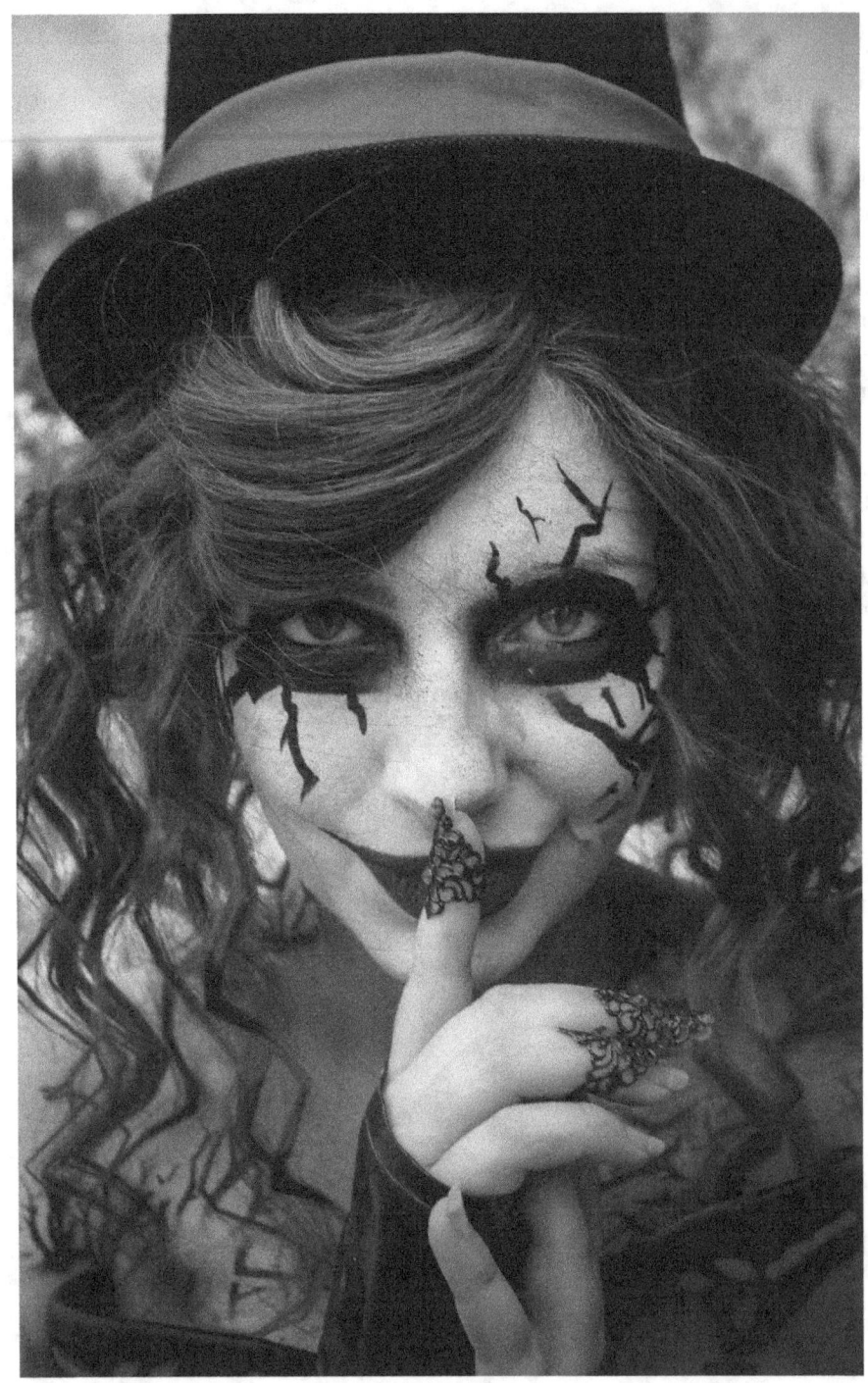

Photographer: Black Rabbit Photography
Model: Miss Mandy Motionless
Designers: Corsettery Corsets, Latexion Design, and Haus De Luxe.
HMUA: Michael Bui

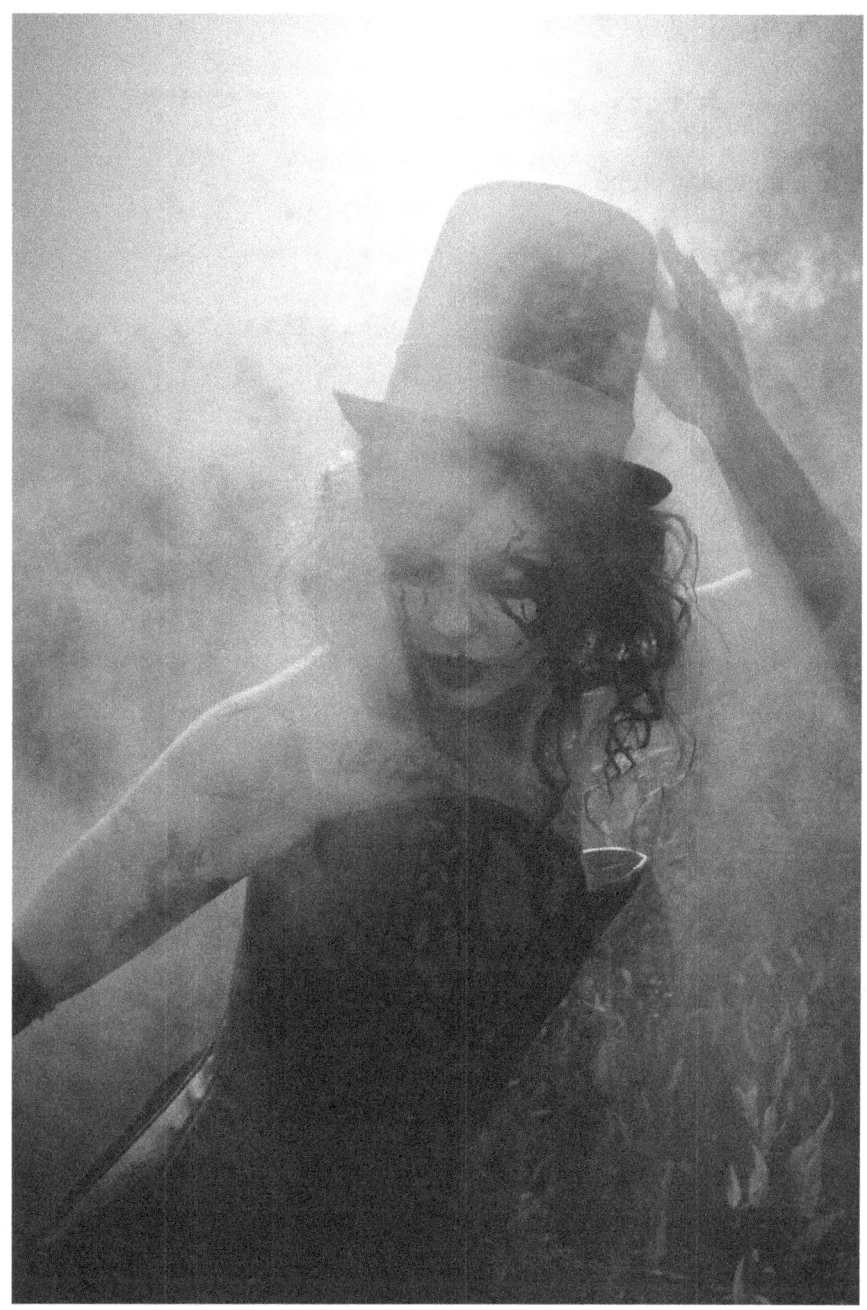

Photographer: Black Rabbit Photography
Model: Miss Mandy Motionless
Designers: Corsettery Corsets, Latexion Design, and Haus De Luxe.
HMUA: Michael Bui

ECHOES OF THE MIND

Painful memories shadow me

like lonesome children, they tag behind

begging me with their winsome smiles,

until I relent and give them shelter

saying, "There, there, it's all right,"

in soothing tones, I hold them close

and cherish their special feeling

for a time, until I remember

the vague, uneasy discomfort

of fingerprints smudging my soul,

forcing me into the still darkness

of my mind, unable to close ranks

as powerful images replicate like a virus,

a mantra of negation chanted, over and over,

until I can no longer think, no longer hear

myself, shamed into silence.

– Julie Bloss Kelsey

dream tiger

swallows
me

swallows me
whole
eats my words

(Head with Shawl, 1912)

your hair

my shawlcover me
with your mouth

my dark
dark flower

(Fiery Head, 1912)

flame of cheek

I cannot touch
your noon

full on
eyes out
of the tunneled dark

(Girl with Doll, 1912)

you hold

to one side
your spitting image

dangling doll
who
holds who

– *Kath Abela Wilson*

The Match

he would not let anyone touch it
after a long walk in the woods
it had embedded itself in his eyelid
with all its strength and beauty

leaning over him
I pulled at the skin gently
leave it there forever
he said

on the threshold
neither in nor out
perhaps he had already relinquished
normality to his dreams

he imagined and accepted a strange future
looking from one eye only
the other closed decoratively like the cover
of a book on natural history

various endeavors of mine
were considered kind but unenlightened
and unsuccessful we settled into the static
nature of the emergency

we waited
until everyone had left the waiting room
to light the last straw
and let it go

– *Kath Abela Wilson*

Another Garden
In response to Marina Tsvetaeva's Sad (Garden)

You'll see the sign that says *50 ahead*.
Make your way across the little bridge:
white rails at the side,
where poplars climb,
new leaves sparkling,
filled with silver eyes.
Willows on the banks will dangle
green dreadlocks
through their shadows in a stream.

Creak as iron gates open.
Recollect the scent
of fresh-turned earth from long ago,
and marble figures
staring on the lawns.
Within an empty chapel,
hear the choir's anthem
drifting through the open door.
Notice granite, carefully inscribed.

Around the gravel, grasses will be trimmed--
The gardener likes to exercise his scythe.

_____

* Silver eyes: tiny Australian songbirds

– *Hazel Hall*

Exemptions will be available for purchase

Good news. New legislation has just been passed. All animals will be recognized as sentient beings. They'll be assigned legal rights like humans including space on earth to live and multiply.

Where humans or animals are deemed by the government to be in plague proportions, euthanasia will be practised to ensure that enough resources and space are available for all. The PM has assured all citizens that this will be fair and accountable. Those to go will be determined by ballot from two groups defined as being:

(a) sick or suffering.
(b) elders
(c) any others draining government resources.

Exemptions will include politicians and humans and animals making major contributions to the economy. In addition, some exemptions will be available for purchase to raise government revenue.

Any human being offering voluntary euthanasia will be rewarded by a generous government grant to surviving relatives.

animal farm
a sty full of pigs
with wings

– Hazel Hall

rewriting the rules
to see
what happens . . .

around the corner
a couple flirts

with nakedness

changing your name
does nothing for fortune

the bright lights
burn down
to a single

bulb

– Peter Jastermsky

THE RIDE TO RETURN

The ride in the car
from airport to back home:
my belly swings

the puke is too much too quick
the day ends in head with what
I'd take to get well

erase memories
of love's lonely pace in an
ever burning house

dog-earing pages
of the fragile world I wrote
and caught myself

again and again
gaze through the darkened space
decay with aged trees

– Ram Krishna Singh

SWEET SAVORS

Strayed far from the nest
I'm fed up living with dust
for years fleeting shade

bereft
of melody
of spirit I sink to
the hades of utter loss
I can't

reckon hidden mysteries
I have lost the sea
for a mere cupful

void of patience and
peace now as I touch the breasts
of the field I crave

for a pure breath
native to
my being I search
sweet savors

of love

– Ram Krishna Singh

Peace

The catastrophe was that neither one was listening. The cacophony was almost symphonic but still, neither listened. It was her father versus my mother and we just needed to find a way to shut all of that out. It really was too much. And so it was that each night, after the dust had settled, our imaginative minds would come out of the shadows to play.

As the lion and lioness settled down at the far end of the house, we would start our late-night sneak. We would meet in her room, quiet as a pair of mice. There we would kiss and touch our way into a state of blissful denial. You can call that what you will. Call it survival, call it escape or you can simply call it peace.

first blossom…
our whispers wrapped
in sounds of rain

– Richard Grahn

daycare provider –
some kids she loves
more than others

migrating birds –
his other personality
comes home from the bar

you pour your anger
into the eggs –
pickled again

– Susan Burch

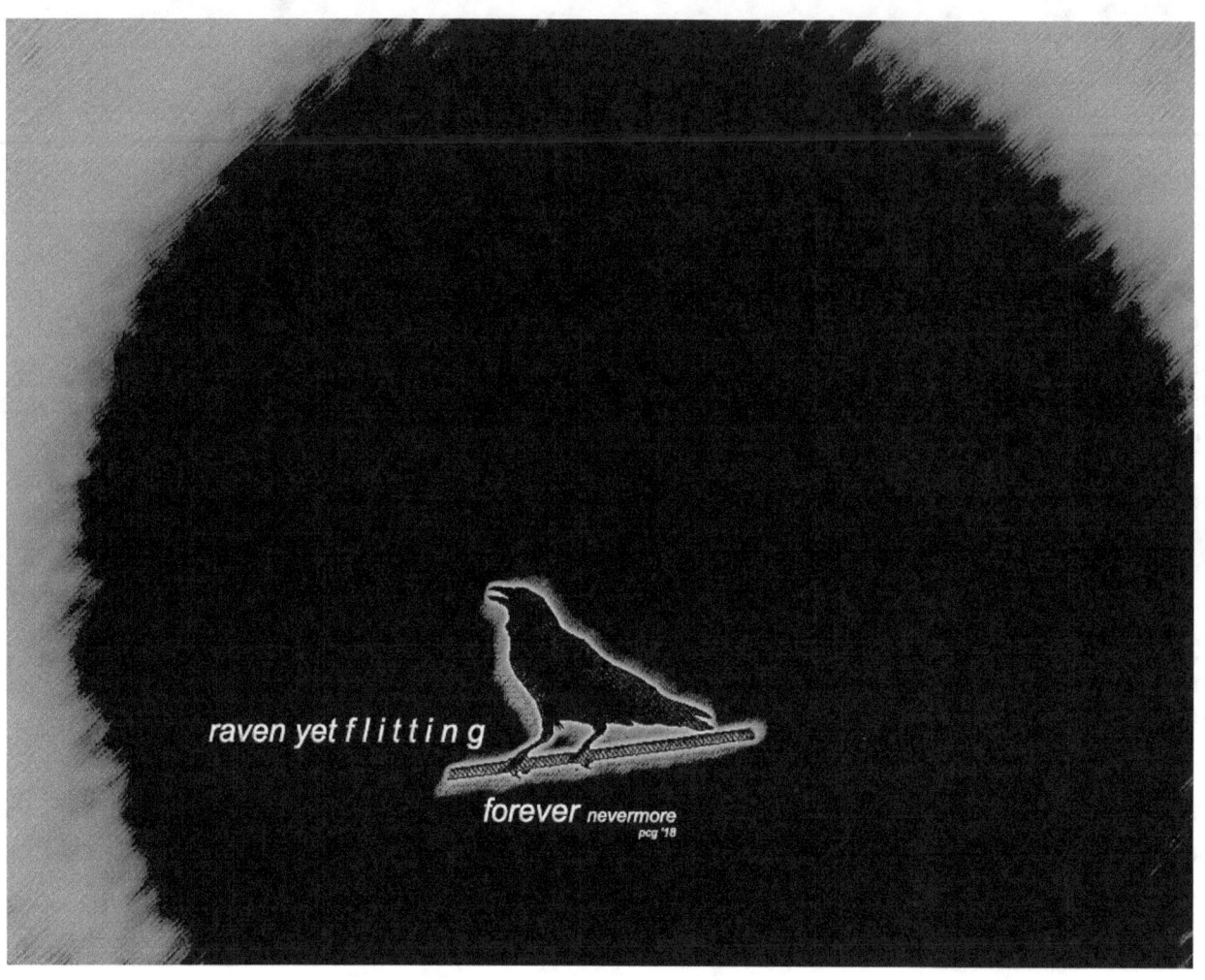

raven yet flitting

forever nevermore
pcg '18

– Pat Geyer

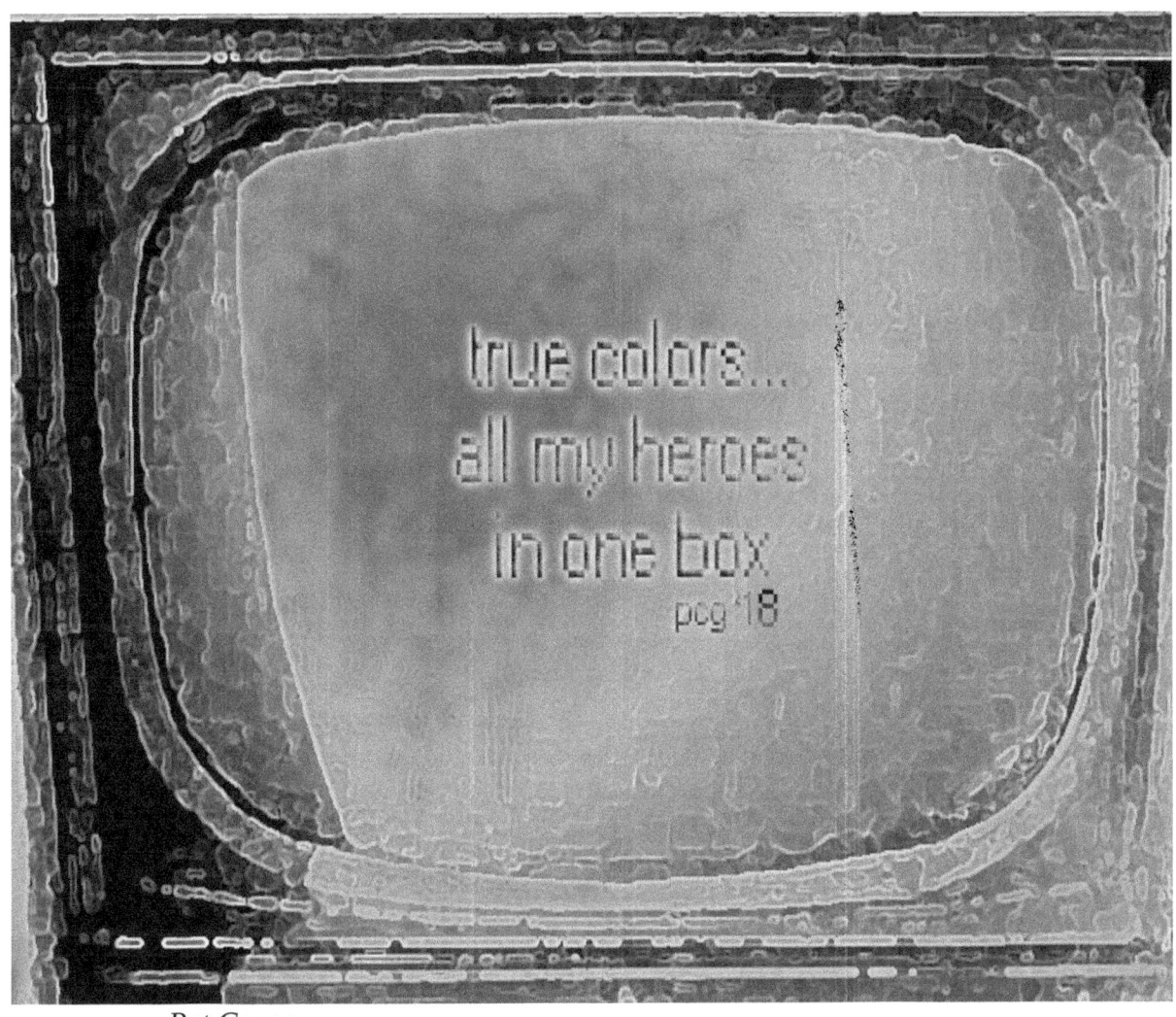

true colors...
all my heroes
in one box
pcg '18

– *Pat Geyer*

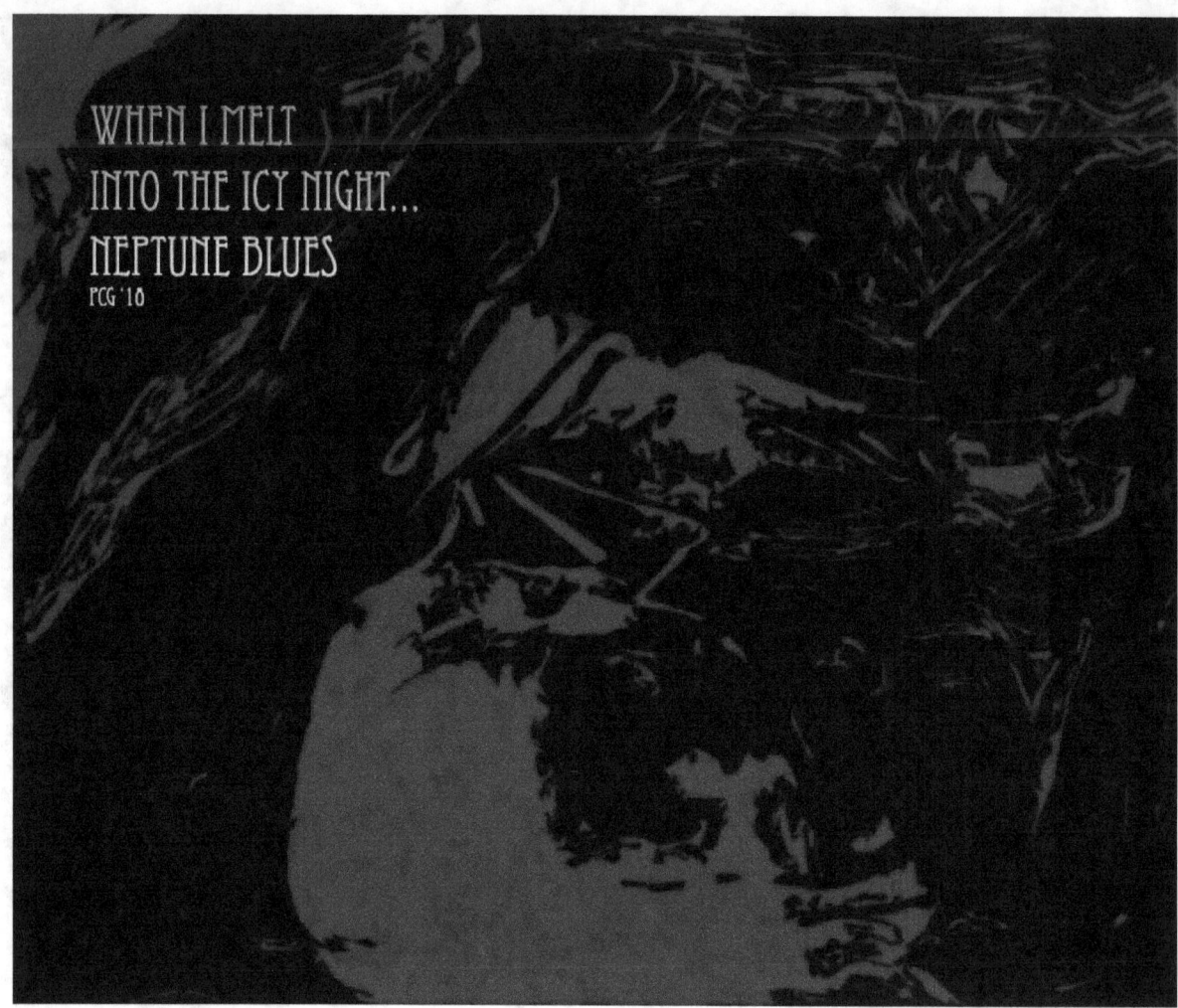

WHEN I MELT
INTO THE ICY NIGHT...
NEPTUNE BLUES
PCG '10

– Pat Geyer

Canis Amica

I see him kick the dog
The yelp carries for blocks
Then he runs down the street
Arms flailing, like a mad man
I am no vigilante, but I take chase
As I gain ground on the fiend
My adrenaline goes crazy
He suddenly stops short
And pulls out a gun
Before I can react
I hear a shot ring out
It hits me in the chest
As I fall to the ground
The dog runs up, limping
And licks my wound
A second shot rings out
It hits the dog in the left eye
But he keeps licking my wound
We die together
Man's best friend and me

– Michael H. Lester

A Big Nothing

The porcupines
Encountered skunks
Quills versus stink
Counter-circles
Worrisome looks
Grunts, snorts, and groans
Discretion wins
Rodents retreat
Mammals split off

Nothing left but
Piles of pellets
Still stinking of
The fear of death
And puddles of
Steaming urine
Dripping down legs
Prancing away
As if it were

A big nothing

– Michael H. Lester

to the fallen muse
whose song is lost in seaweed
wisps of tangled thoughts
diffuse and scattered phrases
of the forsaken poet

as I swing
from the white man's oak
I sing
swing low, sweet chariot
until my neck snaps

sentient beings
from another galaxy
wisely avoid Earth
where people kill each other
and befoul the air they breathe

– Michael H. Lester

spring river
a bag of cats
comes to the surface

hydrant flush
the screams
of missing children

a good shot
the sniper's
sunlit grave

the poetry of hanging

[t]
r
o
p
e

– LeRoy Gorman

Squelch Him

He composes horror music
in the middle of the night
His shadow is large
this master of disguise
and illusion
With a vivid imagination
and snarling voice
He tried to convince me
he was a puppet maker
and I was his marionette
Looking him in the eye
I startled him
Fear has a large shadow
but he himself is quite
small

- Carol Raisfeld

Satan's Scene

Endless nights in eerie lights
souls in shadows broken
on crooked streets, pounding beats
dripping devil's potion
seeing souls of Satan scream
inside his crimson flame
eternally embalmed in fear
and filled with gnawing shame
where the only sound with meaning
is the sound of silent screaming

As days of dreaded doom unroll
in Satan's Pawnshop of the soul
the caverns of my mind explode
with sounds of final feeling
the shattered visions in the road
leave nothing left to see or hold
but a lifeless echo fleeing
a tattered tribute to my being

- Carol Raisfeld

Too Late to Play

Yesterday's playground
now a cage
with carousel music
distorted with age
spinning 'round
too fast to stop
end over end
no bottom no top

Flying too high
in tempo and time
floating on down
trying to climb
with no more space
to right the wrong
buried forever
in sorrow and song

Remember the sights
the smells and the sounds
too late to play
here in the ground

- Carol Raisfeld

Night Rain

unheard prayer
up there somewhere . . .
space junk

paidir nár éisteadh léi
thuas ansin áit éigin . . .
bruscar spáis

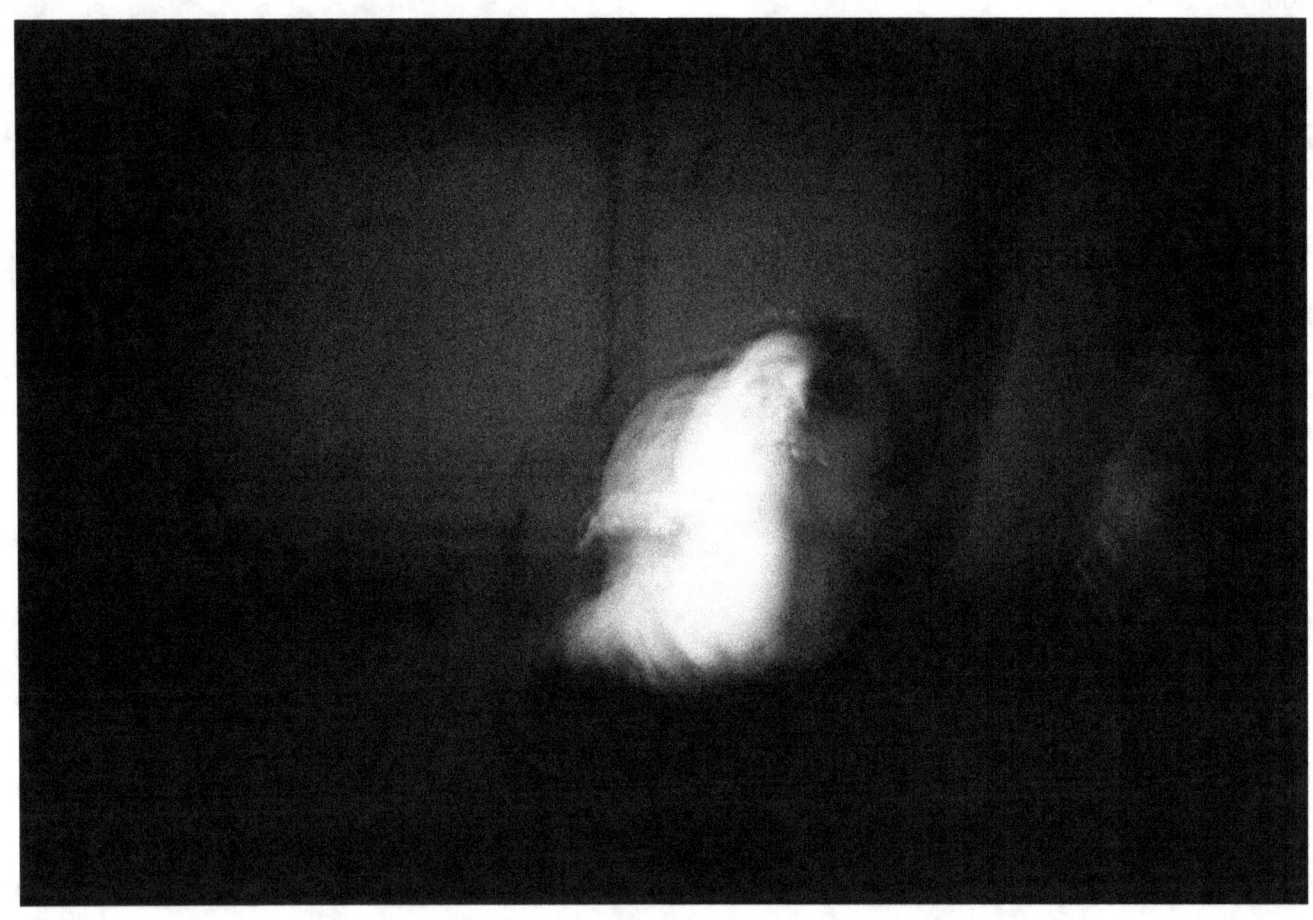

– Haiku by Gabriel Rosenstock, Photography by Debiprasad Mukherjee

strange fruit indeed . . .
my ghost hangs
from a tree

toradh aisteach go deimhin . . .
mo thaise féin
crochta de chrann

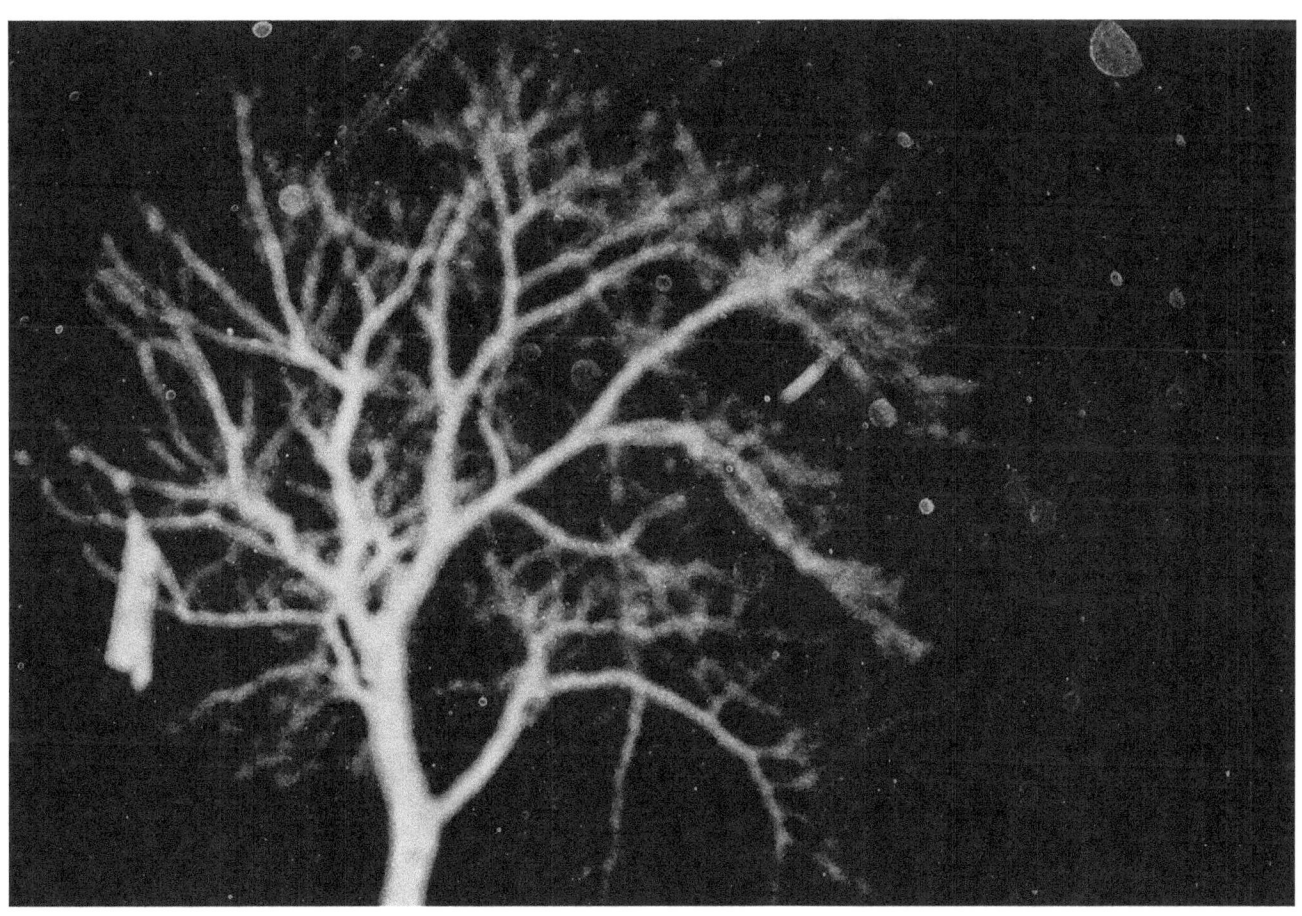

– Haiku by Gabriel Rosenstock, Photography by Debiprasad Mukherjee

shrine	scrín
built for a ghost . . .	a tógadh do thaibhse . . .
the wind dies down	síothlaíonn an ghaoth

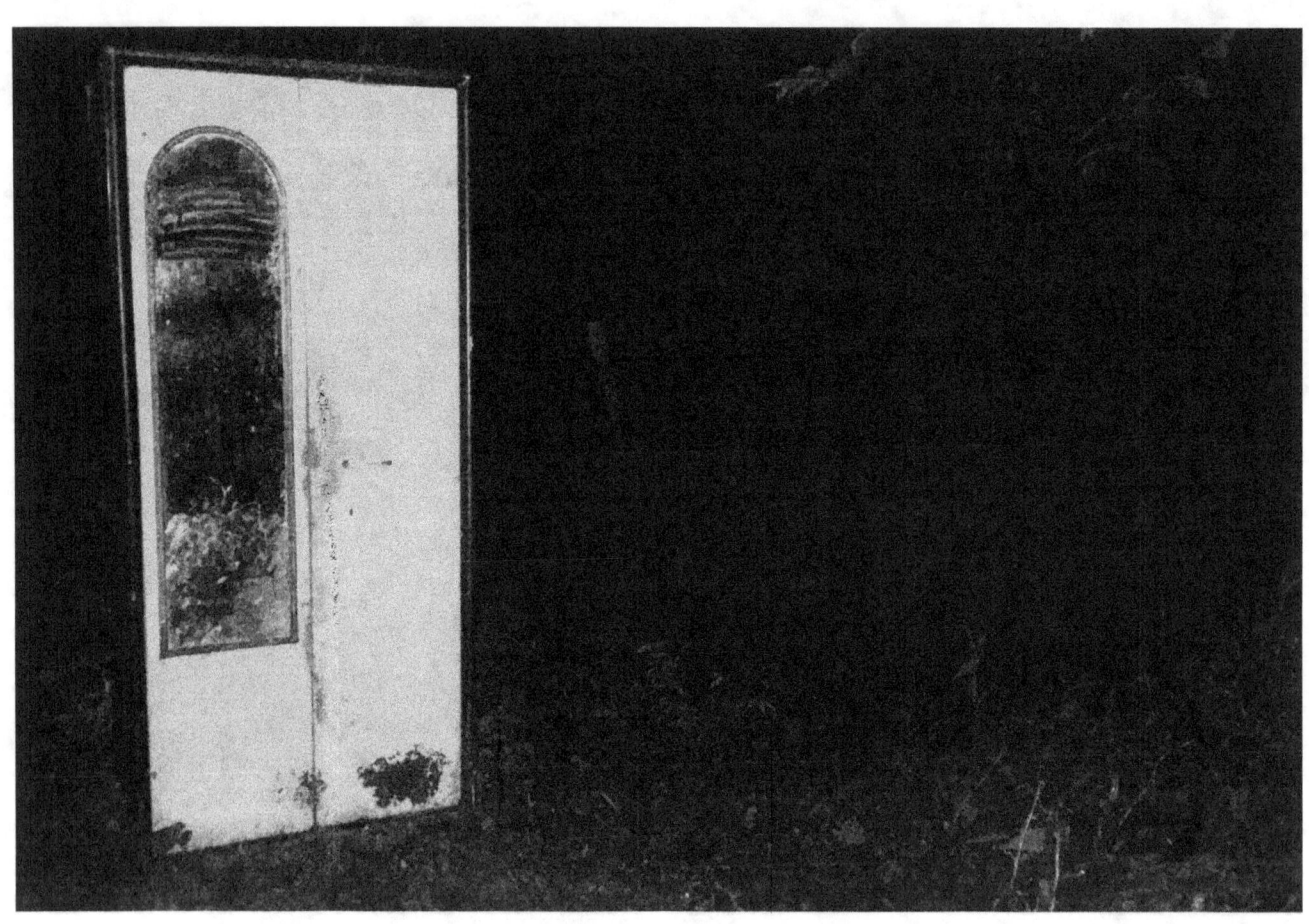

– Haiku by Gabriel Rosenstock, Photography by Debiprasad Mukherjee

night rain .. .
stagnant waters of the mind
come alive

báisteach oíche . . .
beocht athuair in uiscí marbha
na haigne

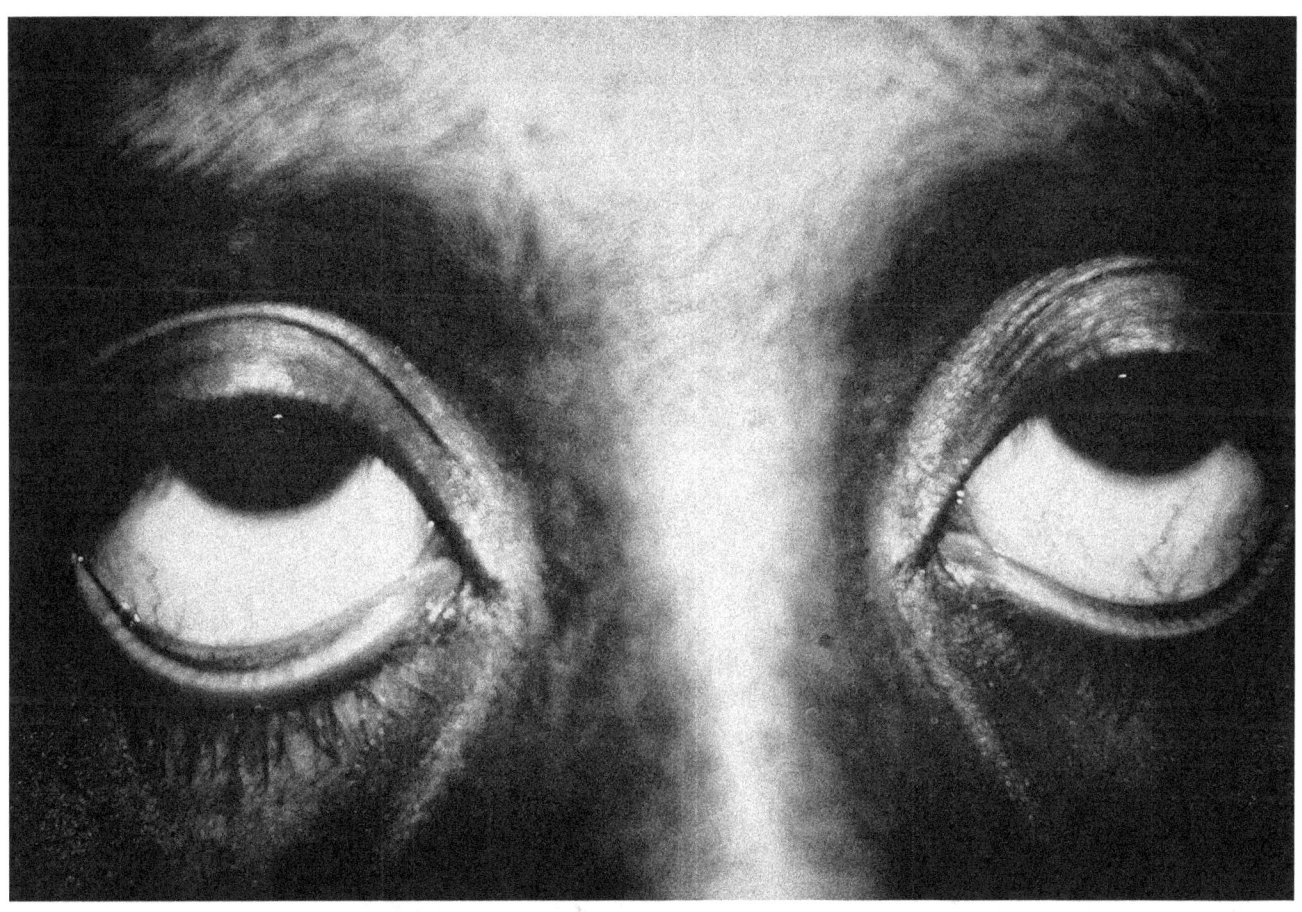

– Haiku by Gabriel Rosenstock, Photography by Debiprasad Mukherjee

litlle skulls
around Kali's neck . . .
counting them

blaoscanna beaga
timpeall mhuineál Chailí . . .
á gcomhaireamh

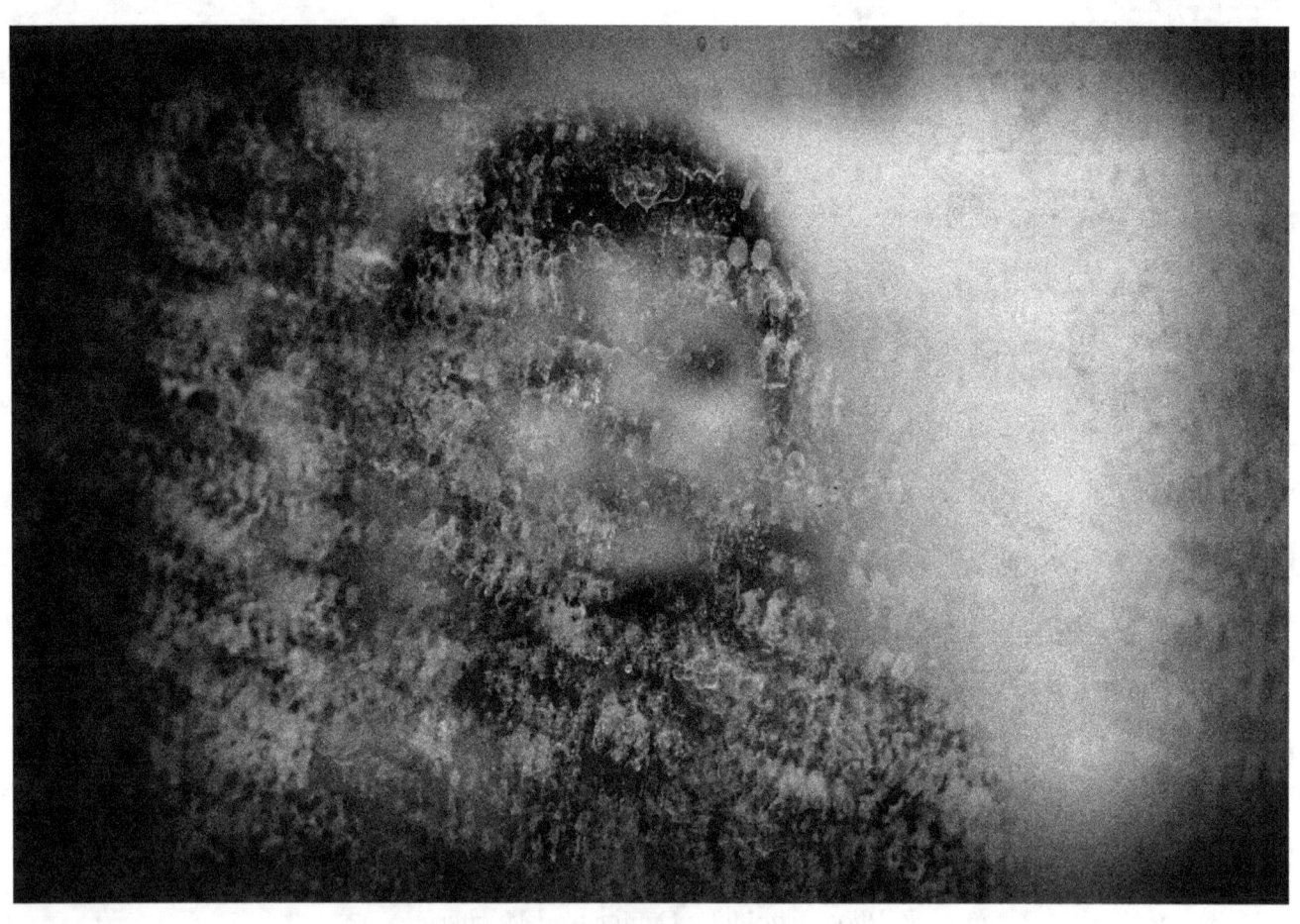

– Haiku by Gabriel Rosenstock, Photography by Debiprasad Mukherjee

The Dragon of Orleans

It was a night of heat in New Orleans. The lone man carrying his belongings in a pack upon his back walked the streets of the dark city. He seemed drawn to a large house at the end of a dark road. The area was near the edge of the city, but it seemed strangely isolated from the world. A black swamp lay about the building only grudgingly allowing the road to approach the dark structure. In this moonless night, it appeared as if moss made up the walls of the ancient home. A great tree hovered above the house, seemingly forming part of the roof. Above the porch a green neon light flashed "Luz's Bar and Grill".

The man walked up a set of dark wet steps and into an empty room, except for one man standing behind a long mahogany bar. Tables and booths filled the remainder of the room. The man seemed to move in total silence across the bar to a small booth in a dim corner. He sat his pack on the seat across the booth and settled onto the other bench seat. The large, black bartender looked over at the muscular, white man sitting in the darkened corner. Slowly walking around the bar, he approached the booth to take the man's order.

"What would you like?" he asked in a deep, powerful and somewhat unfriendly voice.

"Do you have food?" the man asked in a gentle, but powerful tone.

"We have the best gumbo in Orleans."

"Can you make it hot?"

"Any heat you want."

"I want it hot enough to kill." The man said as he stroked the green stone that held down several cloth coasters in the center of the table.

"I think, I can accommodate you. Anything to drink?"

"Eight ounces of straight bourbon."

"Alright, any brand you like?" the man asked with a suspicious tone in his voice.

"Walker," the unusual man said.

The bartender walked back to the bar and talked to someone through a window in the back wall. When the bartender looked back, the stone upon the table had started to glow, but the white man didn't seem to notice the gentle glow. He pressed a button under the bar top and then poured the bourbon. A slim, tall and beautiful, jet black woman walked out of a back room.

"Something wrong?" she asked the bartender.

"The stone," he said in a whisper as he nodded toward the man.

She looked over and smiled. Taking the drink the woman walked over to the booth.

"Here's your drink. May I sit?" she asked in an unusually sultry voice.

"Please," he said and opened his hand toward the other side of the booth.

"I'm the owner, Luz," she said pushing the pack aside and sitting down. She watched the man shake hot sauce into his bourbon, something she'd never seen before. "You've never been here before."

"No, it's my first time in New Orleans. I travel a lot and this time I ended up here."

As he took a sip from the glass his shirt fell open a bit, revealing a glowing eye on the man's chest. She could just make out the head of a dragon, but it was more than a tattoo. It looked almost alive. She could swear the glowing eye was staring at her. He quickly adjusted his shirt to cover the image once again.

"What's your name?" Luz asked.

"Zachariah Will, call me Zak."

"Nice to meet you," she held out her hand. As he grasped it, she felt a heat emanating from his skin. It was like he had a high fever, but he looked fine, even a bit pale. "The stone you're handling is glowing." Luz pointed out to the man.

"It's just the light in here," the man said pulling his hand from the crystal, causing its glow to fade. Luz knew it was not the bar's light. She had placed the colored crystals on the tables, to see if any would glow in the presence of one of her patrons. He was the first to cause any of the stones to react.

"Where are you headed?" she asked the man.

"I come from nowhere and I'm going nowhere," he answered, in all honesty.

"I see. So you have no plans?"

"Only to find a place to stay tonight."

"I may be able to help you with that. I have rooms for rent on the third floor."

"How much? I'm a little lean on money at the moment."

"Do you need a job?"

"Well, it would help. I usually find a few construction jobs here and there. You see I'm a carpenter."

"If you're interested, I have some work out back."

"Well, let me look at it." Zak said as he stood and offered his hand to help Luz get out of the booth.

Luz hit a switch on the wall as they walked through a set of double doors onto an old wooden deck. Flood lights illuminated the deck and a field beyond. As they walked across the deck it creaked and moved slightly. It was large enough for fifty or so people, but he could tell it was about to collapse.

The deck overlooked a two-hundred foot deep, grassy field, which ended in a dark, rather ugly swamp. He saw hundreds of dead trees with Spanish moss hanging from their lifeless limbs. The whole area was covered by dark undulating black water. A rotted, partially collapsed, wooden fence separated the grassy field from the swamp.

"Do you want the fence replaced?"

"No, don't touch the fence, but you could put a new fence about ten feet in front of the old."

"You sure you don't want it torn down?"

"No, don't go near it," Luz repeated.

"Is there a problem?"

"It's a long story."

"I have all the time in the world." Zak said as he carefully leaned on the rickety banister.

"Well, about a hundred years ago the most powerful voodoo priest in the city built this house. He had a beautiful daughter who was to be married. In the swamp lived a family that was known to be wild and savage. They lived off the bounty of the swamp and seldom came into Orleans.

"The daughter of the priest was sitting on a stone patio that lay below this deck. Two of the sons from the swamp family took her. When the girls father returned he found a scene of struggle, violence and blood. An amulet known to be owned by one of the sons was found and the priest called upon his followers to search for his daughter. She was found a few hours later, just inside the swamp. She had been raped and beaten. A week later she died from her injuries. The swamp was searched, but they could not find the family.

"The girl's father called together all the voodoo priests and priestesses in Orleans. They stood in a circle, in the field you're looking over. They called upon the darkest of powers. At midnight, upon the new moon, a hideous curse was placed upon the family. They would forever after remain in the swamp. Death would come upon them only if the sun's rays touched their skin. A curse was also placed on the swamp, driving out all life except for vermin. Some say there are nights you can hear the swamp family's moans of despair. On moonlit nights, dark shapes can be seen moving aimlessly among the dead trees." Luz told him, looking at the swamp.

"You believe this?"

"Yes, yes I do," she said in all seriousness. The man simply smiled and shock his head slightly.

"I can rebuild the deck and put up a new fence. It will take several months and I will need some money for materials."

"How much will you charge me?"

"Room and board and a couple of hundred dollars when I finish."

"Done," she said, as they shook hands.

Within a month he had torn down the old deck and built a new support structure. Zak had also erected the fence posts along the back of the property, while never touching the old fence, as Luz requested. He always wore a long sleeve shirt that fully covered his chest. Luz notice he seemed to never sweat and the heat seemed to mean nothing to him. It was as if he had been raised in hell itself. He worked steadily for ten to twelve hours a day, never stopping or getting tired. Each night he ate in the bar, always asking for the food to be made hotter and with more spice than the night before.

One night the cook decided to teach Zak a lesson and he cooked four whole ghost peppers in the man's chili. The cook had seen men collapse to their knees from the heat, with just one such pepper in their food. As the cook and the bartender watched, the man ate the chili without even noticing the heat. The bartender walked over and picked up the empty bowl. Zak looked up and said, "I see the cook finally got a little spice in the chili. I'd like another bowl and a bit more heat would be nice."

The bartender told the cook what Zak had said. The cook went back to the kitchen. He put plastic gloves on and took the ten remaining peppers and chopped them, seeds and all, into a small mince. Then the entire ten peppers were put into the bowl of chili and mixed in. The cook decided to see if the peppers were truly hot, so he put a small piece left on the chopping board onto the tip of his tongue. It took several seconds before he felt the heat. It was as if a hole was being burnt through his tongue. He stumbled to the cooler and managed to get to a gallon jug of milk. After he drank half the milk, the heat finally began to subside. Luz came into the kitchen and saw the chili. Picking up a spoon, she was about to sample it, when the chef choked out, "Don't, it will burn your stomach out!"

She turned to him holding a spoon of chili before her, "What?"

"I put ten ghost peppers in it," he croaked out, still feeling the heat.

"Are you crazy? Whoever eats this could die." He then explained what had happened. She looked at him like he was insane and took the bowl with her. Luz walked to Zak and explained what had happened. He took the bowl from her and as she watched Zak finished all the chili without breaking a sweat.

"How can you eat that?" she asked in amazement.

"As long as I can remember I haven't been able to taste anything but extremely hot and spicy food."

"It must be bothersome not to be able to taste anything but highly spicy food."

"It is a bit."

"Could you be finished with the work on the deck in four weeks?"

"Yes, I should be able to. Is there some reason for the time line?"

"On the full moon of next month, it will be a hundred years since the curse was put on the family. It's thought that the curse will be at its weakest upon that night and some believe the family will try to break out of the swamp using their own black magic. I'm planning for a lot of customers to show up to see if anything happens. They'll want to use the deck to watch the swamp."

"I see," he said, laughing a bit at what people were willing to turn into a party.

The weeks passed as Zak slowly completed the fence and then the deck. Luz had begun to have dinner each night with Zak and had started to truly care about this odd man. She suspected that he also cared for her. Finally, the deck was completed just one day before the hundred-year anniversary of the curse. Zak said he would stay for the festivities, but would be leaving the next morning. Luz planned to offer him a permanent job after "The Party of the Dark Swamp", was over. She was hoping to keep him with her.

Luz inspected the work and it was unlike any carpentry she had ever seen. There was not a single nail or screw used. Everything was held together with wood pins. The structure seemed as solid as a rock. It looked as if it was built two hundred years earlier, except the wood was all new. The deck had the feeling of an old sailing-vessel.

Zak came into the bar just as the first customers were arriving. By eleven thirty that evening. the bar was packed and the new deck was filling up in anticipation of the breaking of the curse. Luz was the perfect hostess, making sure all were served with food and drink. People were awaiting midnight when it was thought the family would try to break out of the swamp. Most believed nothing would happen, but came for the fun of the thing. The full, bright moon lit the field and the new fence with an odd glow.

As midnight arrived, a loud screeching was heard from the swamp and then an unusual pounding came from the darkness beyond the new fence. Suddenly, two of the fence panels seemed to explode into the grassy field. six dark figures slowly came through the gaping hole in the fence. A stray dog, that Luz had been feeding, rushed barking and snarling toward the lurching creatures. The animal grabbed the leg of one of the creatures. It reached down, lifting the dog off the ground, as two other creatures grabbed the dog's back legs. With one vicious pull, they tore the dog's legs off. The animal howled in pain as the first creature crushed its skull killing the animal. A number of the women fainted on the deck, while others screamed as all felt a ghastly fear descend upon them.

The creatures tore at the remains of the dog's body and feed on the dog's remains. After finishing their feast they once again started to move towards the deck. Luz saw Zak jump from the deck, landing in front of the advancing figures. He looked toward the creatures then his back began to arch as he fell to his knees. Zak's upper body curved back toward the ground as his chest pointed to the sky. Suddenly, he screamed in pain as his shirt burst into flame and burned away from his body revealing a startling red, glowing dragon etched upon his chest. Heat rose from the dragon's figure forming a red mist above the man. The mist drifted up as the dragon figure seemed to blur on Zak's chest. The red mist rose into the sky and spread out until it was as wide as the house and twice as tall. The mist, then started to solidify as the dragon figure disappeared from his chest. Large red wings formed from the mist and then a great body came into existence. Next, a huge spiked head and finally a long tail that ended on Zak's chest formed. The tail separated from his body as the great flying beast looked at those standing upon the deck. Its red glow lighted the ground and sky. Everyone flinched back as hideous screeches came from the dark creatures advancing upon the deck. The dragon twisted in the air and looked to the sound.

The creatures had backed away from the dragon and formed into a tight group. They then grasped each others hands and reached into the air. A dark cloud formed above them. A black bolt of lightning came from the cloud, striking the dragon on its chest. The great beast howled in pain and its eyes began to swirl in blood-red anger. It then breathed in, filling its massive chest with air. From its great maw came a blast of red fire that struck the group of creatures with such force that the ground shook. The intense heat singed the hair and clothes of the people standing on the deck and blistered the paint upon the house.

As the flame died, the creatures were gone, leaving nothing but a blacken circle on the ground. Luz looked back at Zak and he seemed frozen in the same arched position. She then heard more screeching from the swamp. The dragon apparently heard the same sounds and flew up into the sky. It then dove down toward the swamp curving its flight as it approached the leading edge of the swamp. A great blast of dragon fire burst upon the dead water covered land. The trees did not simply catch on fire, they disintegrated. The black water below them boiled into a dark steam.

The dragon swooped up and dove again and again. Each time burning out a section of the swamp. When the flying beast finished, the swamp was nothing more than a huge, burnt out pit. Nothing stood, nothing survived. The house stood alone with its few living trees among before the blacken earth of the once dark swamp. The glowing red dragon then flew high into the sky until it almost disappeared from sight. Finally, it dove toward the ground, directly at Zak.

The dragon's form blurred as its shape changed from a great, solid body into a stream of bright red mist. The mist struck Zak's chest entering his body like water pouring into a glass. Luz watched the dragon figure reappear upon his chest as the last of the mist flowed into his body. His body unfroze and fell back onto the grass. There he lay on his side, utterly still as if dead.

Near the front of the deck Luz climbed onto the seat of a built-in booth. She clapped her hands above her head and the sound instantly penetrated through the crowd. They looked to the tall, black women standing above them. Luz clasped her hands above her head and they began to glow a yellowish green color. All in the crowd were mesmerized by the light.

"Listen," she said in a loud, but melodious spell-binding voice. "This night, no creatures came from the swamp, no dragon flew through the skies. What you saw was a great lightning bolt striking one of the dead trees within the swamp. The tree exploded into flames, which then raged across the swamp creating an inferno. The all-consuming fire and intense heat utterly destroyed all life within the swamp. That is what you have seen this evening and that is what you shall remember! Now it is time to leave this place and return to your homes. Remember the lightning, remember the great swamp fire, remember nothing else."

Luz lowered her hands as the glow faded. The people before her stood unmoving for a few moments. Then, slowly they came back to themselves and began to walk toward the doors. Luz could hear the comments of the crowd as she rushed across the deck, to the stairway that led to the field below.

"Did you ever see lightning like that?"

"Man, that fire was incredible. You could feel the heat. It felt like my hair was on fire."

"Did you feel the deck shake when the lightning hit?"

Luz reached Zak and slowly straightened his legs. She then carefully pulled him onto his back. The vivid red dragon stared up at her, unblinking from his chest. He was breathing normally, but was unconscious. She heard something behind her and looked over her shoulder. There stood the bartender looking down at the two.

"Is he dead?" the huge man asked.

"No, just unconscious. Let's get him to my bedroom."

"Yes, ma'am," he said picking up the man with great difficultly.

Zak awoke and slowly opened his eyes. His sight cleared gradually to reveal a tall woman silhouetted against a large brightly lit window. She appeared to be looking into the sky and enjoying the light.

"How long has it been?" he asked in a hoarse voice.

"Two days," Luz replied without turning.

"Where are they?" Zak asked.

"Where are who?"

"The reporters, the law," he replied.

"There will be no reporters, no law. Those who were here that night only remember a lightning strike that started an inferno that destroyed the swamp. You and your friend are safe here."

"How did you manage that?"

"I inherited more than this house. The powers of my ancestors flow within me. I simply suggested that they forget the dragon and remember a fire."

"I see," he said.

"How long have you had the beast on your chest?"

"I was born with it, a long, long time ago. I think you may have had an idea that I was a bit different."

"When you touched the green stone that first night, it glowed."

"Ah, yes, I should have realized," he said with a smile on his face.

"I had no idea what you were capable of," she said as she slowly turned, still in silhouette.

"Where am I? This isn't my room."

"No, it's our room," she said in a sultry voice as she walked out of the light. He could see that she was naked as she slipped into the bed.

"Are you sure about this? I cannot stay forever."

"I know, but for now you are here."

The next morning they were sitting on the deck finishing their breakfast. "I have something to show you just beyond the old fence," she told Zak as she stood. They walked through the hole in the fence, to a large boulder at the separation of the swamp and the field. A greenish water had already filled the burnt out area. The true swamp was taking back what it had lost. Soon the area would be full of life.

She pointed to letters, etched by fire, into a boulder's hard, smooth surface.

"ALL EVIL DIES UPON A DRAGON'S BREATH!"

– *A.D. Adams*

pesticides

your words crawling
under my skin
bed bugs

weaving in and out
of everything you said
spiderwebs

stomping on
my self esteem
cockroaches

the way you suck
the life from me
parasites

shedding you
from my memory
snake skin

– Lori A Minor

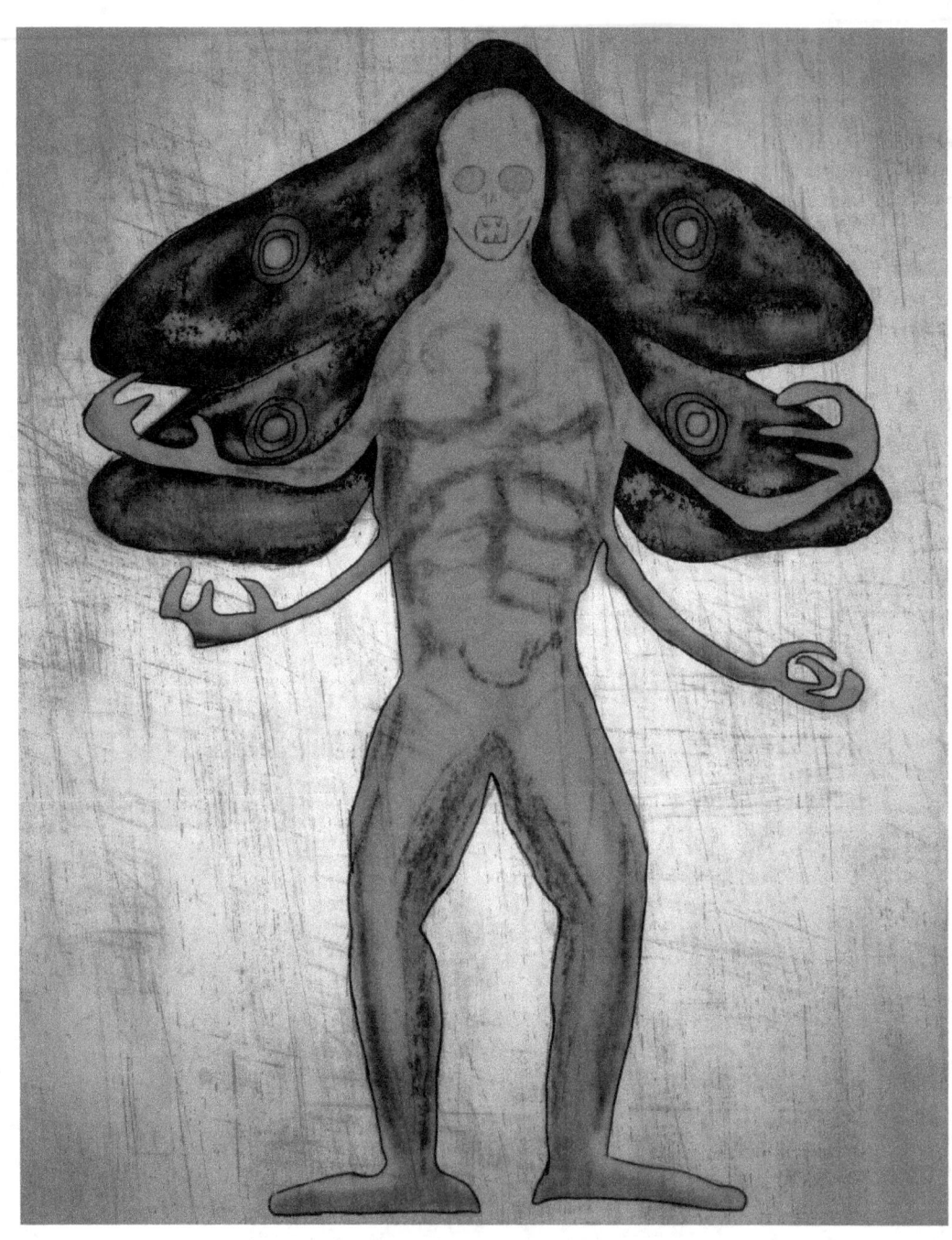

Mothman

– *Lori A Minor*

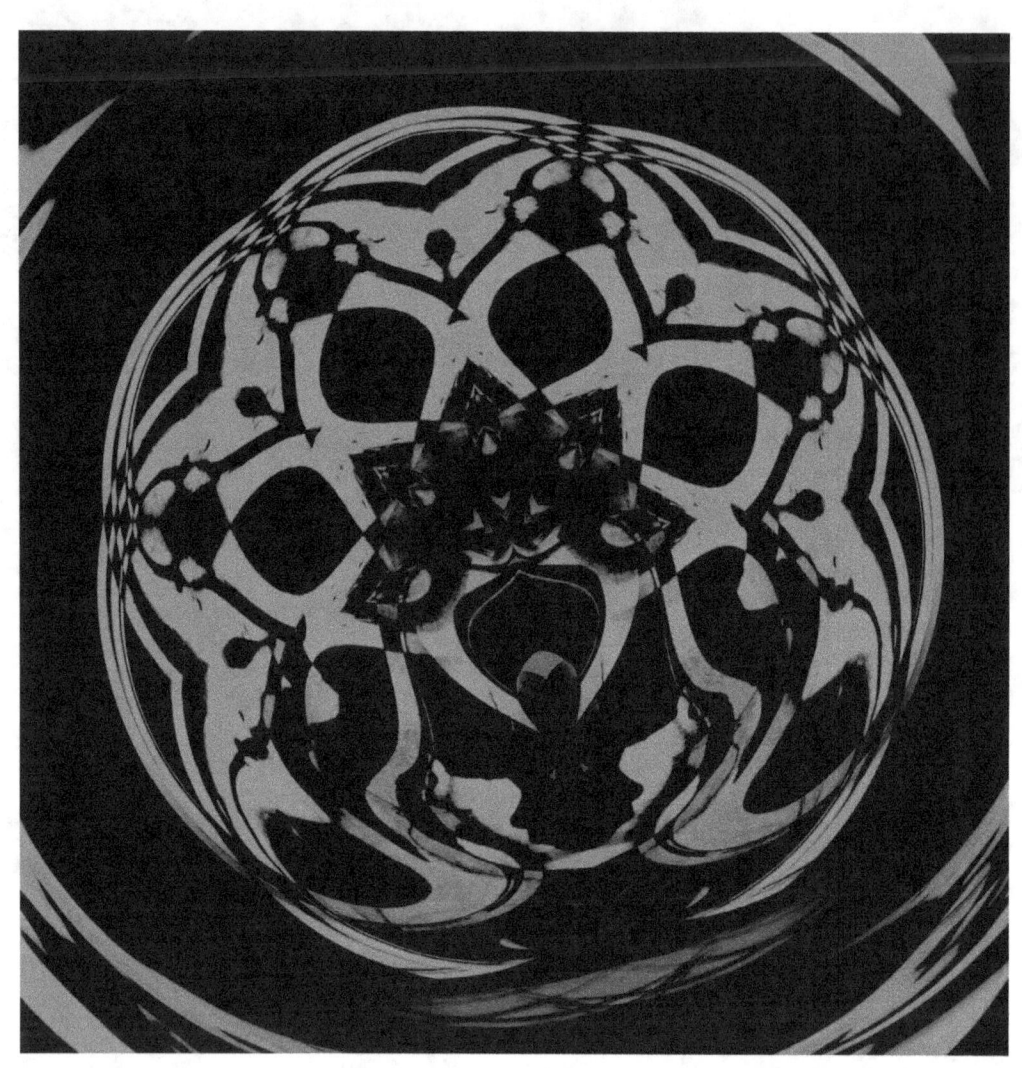

Under His Eye

– Lori A Minor

'Lil Grim

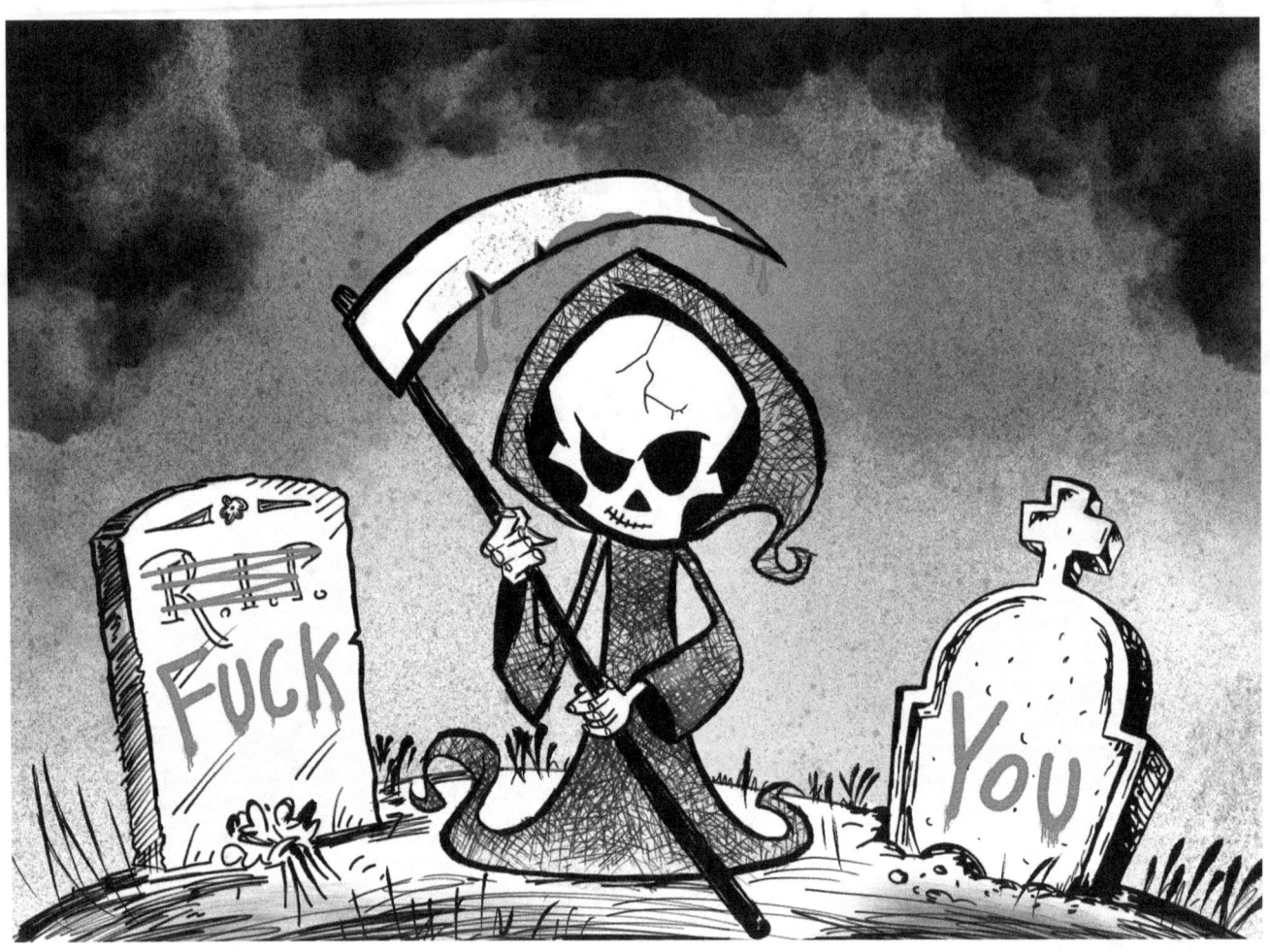

– Chase Gagnon

The Ghost of Minnie Quay

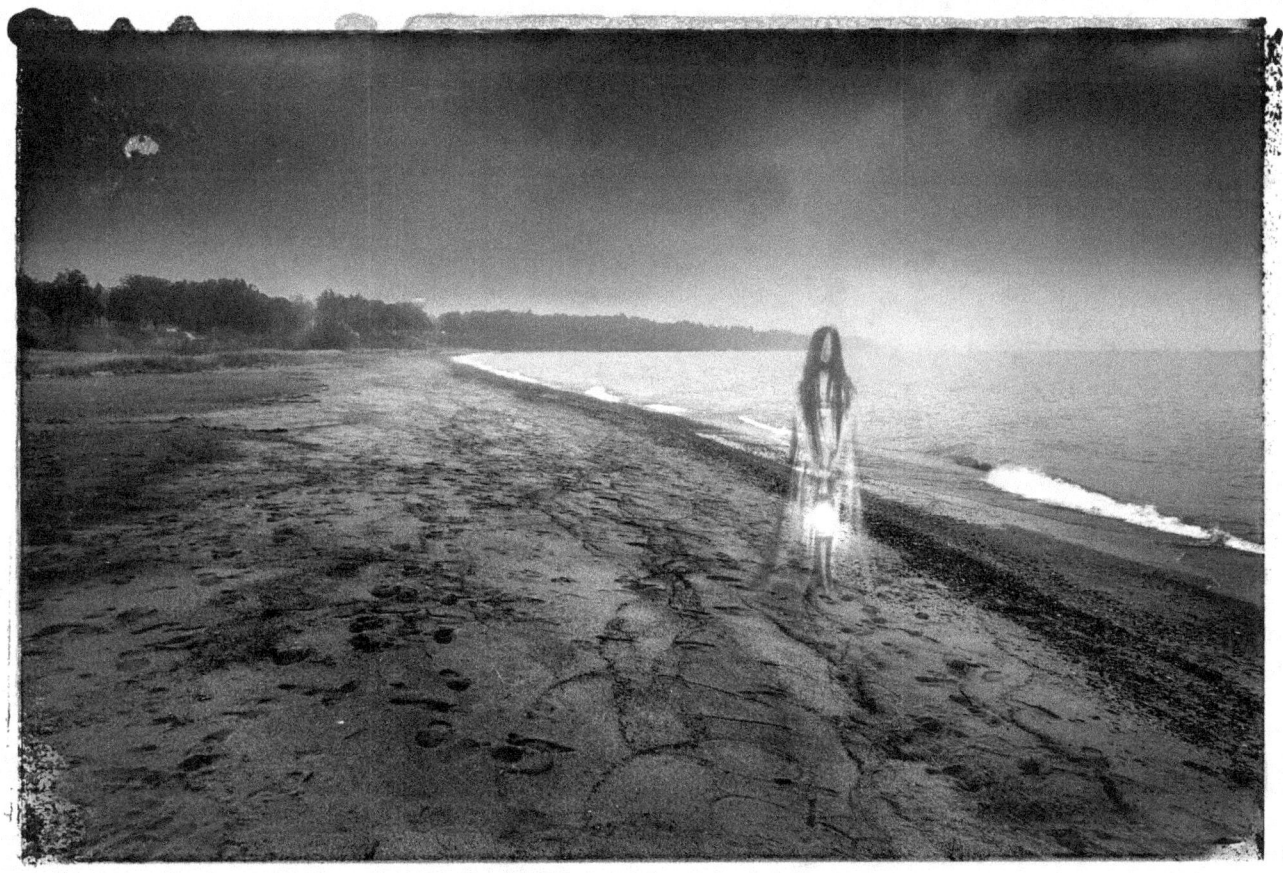

"The Quay family, father James and mother Mary Ann, lived in the busy lumbering town of Forester. Their daughter, Minnie Quay, was only 15 at the time. She had given her heart to a young sailor whose ship would dock in Forester often for either shipping or merchant reasons. Not much is known about the gentleman, only that Minnie had fallen in love with him. Many in town warned her about this affair. Her own mother would often yell out loud enough for others in town to hear that she would rather see her dead than with this man. In the early spring of 1876, word came back to Forester that his ship had gone down in a storm on the Great Lakes of Michigan. Minnie was torn, as her parents had not allowed her to say goodbye the last time he had left town. A few days later, on April 27, her parents gave her charge to watch her younger brother, James Jr. As the infant was sleeping, Minnie walked into town, and passed by the town inn, the Tanner House. People sitting on the porch waved to the young girl as she passed them and walked to the pier. The onlookers watched as she jumped off the pier, into the cold dark waters of Lake Huron.

Her ghost has been said to roam the beaches of Forester. Some have said that she just walks, waiting for her lover to dock, while others have stated that she has tried to beckon young girls into the waters to their deaths."

– *Chase Gagnon*

Malédiction de la Nain Rouge

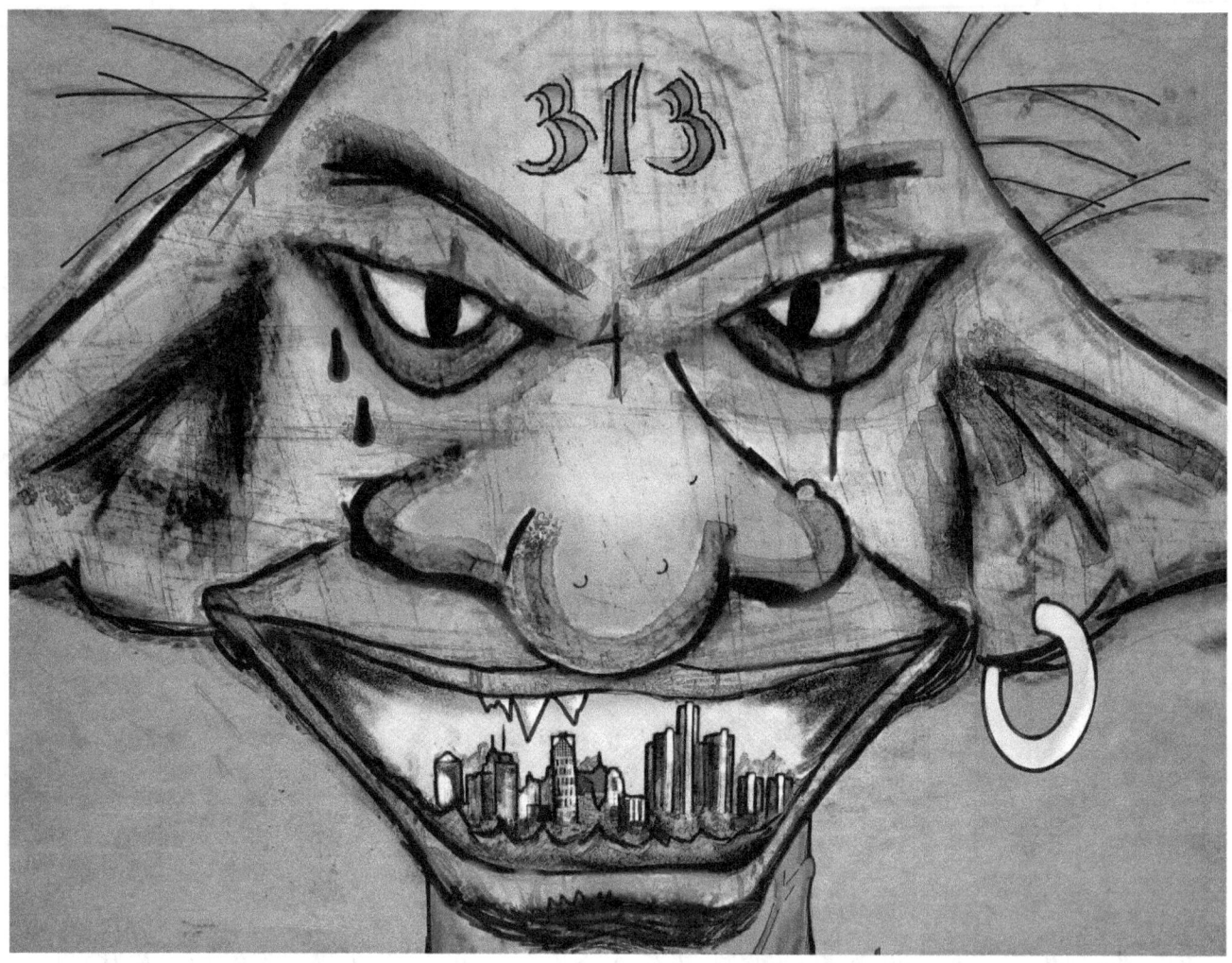

"The Nain Rouge (French for "red dwarf") also called "Demon of the Strait", is a legendary creature of the Detroit, Michigan area whose appearance is said to presage misfortune and destruction. According to various narratives surrounding the figure, Detroit's founder Antoine de la Mothe Cadillac was told by a fortuneteller to appease the Nain Rouge, but upon encountering the creature, he smacked it with his cane and shouted, "Get out of my way, you red imp!" As a consequence, a string of bad luck befell Cadillac; he was charged with abuse of power and reassigned to Louisiana, later returning to France where he was briefly imprisoned and eventually lost his fortune."

– Chase Gagnon

Book Reviews

Flying Free by Rachel Sutcliffe

In Rachel Sutcliffe's collection "Flying Free" we see the strength of the poet on full display. In the introduction, Sutcliffe says that writing has been her therapy and states that "it's kept me from going insane" which in itself is a recipe for brilliant poetry.

Aesthetically, the poetry has a smooth, lyrical feel all throughout the collection which contrasts perfectly with the often somber subject matter of the pieces. There are so very few people in this world can take some of life's greatest challenges turn them into something meaningful – something beautiful. After Reading "Flying Free" I know without a doubt that Rachel Sutcliffe is one of those people.

This is one of the most inspirational collections I've read in a very long time, and I'm sure I'll return to it again and again for years to come.

To read this collection for free, please visit:
https://docs.wixstatic.com/ugd/396b91_08d917b2c53747b59c06d71ec277ee71.pdf

– *Chase Gagnon*
co-editor, Scryptic Magazine

Empty Pockets by Chase Gagnon

Even though I have seen Chase's work a thousand times, I was still blown away when I read Empty Pockets for the first time. My eyes were completely opened as I sifted through and examined each haiga within his book. Not only do you see the blight and renewal of Gagnon's beloved city, but of the poet himself. Not only do you see juxtaposition within each ku, but between the ku and photo, and even the poet and his haiga. Several haiku have the perfect juxtaposition as he compares himself with the grimy, rundown city of Detroit. You can see this in ku such as this one:

>who I used to be. . .
>the empty streets
>of the motor city

If you ask a haijin what haiku in it's purest form means to them, they'll most likely bring up nature and kigo, however Chase Gagnon didn't grow up with that sort of connection to nature. His nature is *urban* and you see that in this poignant poem:

>polluted sky –
>does the wind remember
>the feeling of trees

Gagnon brings to the table a brand new way to view nature, and haiku. Empty Pockets is a waterfall of original material and unlike nothing you've ever seen before. Even if you're familiar with Chase's work, seeing it all combined into one tangible gallery will be something you'll come back to time and time again.

To view some of the haiga in this collection, please visit https://www.youtube.com/watch?v=PVdo-2HV7m0&feature=youtu.be

To purchase your own copy of empty pockets, please visit https://www.amazon.com/Empty-Pockets-Chase-Gagnon/dp/1717354947

– Lori A Minor
co-editor, Scryptic Magazine
editor, #FemkuMag

CALL FOR SUBMISSIONS:

We are putting together a collection of art, poetry, photography, digital art, and short stories titled Group Therapy. This collection of work will be centered around those surviving abuse. Group Therapy was inspired by the various forms of abuse we both have endured and how it has affected us throughout our lives. This project is also intended to help heal those affected by abuse.

Group Therapy will be a free PDF download, but will be put into a print edition for purchase (black and white or color option), just like the issues of Scryptic. Just because your story is not chosen does not mean your story is invalid. We may make suggestions on grammar, form, spelling, etc., but never the context.

Please send any number of poems (all forms), short stories (1.5k words or less), paintings, drawings, digital art, or photography to grouptherapybook@gmail.com

There is no set deadline at this time. Pieces can be published or unpublished. If published, please send publication credits underneath the piece in this format:

Example: Scryptic Magazine, 1.3

This collection is dedicated to those surviving abuse. We will not publish anything that condones abuse, violence, racism, or harm to any person or group of people.

Images sent to this collection may be considered for the cover.